D0010531

Elizabethan Drama

TITLES IN THE
GREENHAVEN PRESS COMPANION TO LITERARY
MOVEMENTS AND GENRES SERIES:

American Modernism
American Realism
American Romanticism
Elizabethan Drama
Greek Drama
Victorian Literature

THE GREENHAVEN PRESS COMPANION TO
Literary Movements and Genres

Elizabethan Drama

Laura K. Egendorf, *Book Editor*

David L. Bender, *Publisher*

Bruno Leone, *Executive Editor*

Bonnie Szumski, *Editorial Director*

David M. Haugen, *Managing Editor*

Greenhaven Press, Inc., San Diego, CA

Every effort has been made to trace the owners of copyrighted material. The articles in this volume may have been edited for content, length, and/or reading level. The titles have been changed to enhance the editorial purpose. Those interested in locating the original source will find the complete citation on the first page of each article.

Library of Congress Cataloging-in-Publication Data

Elizabethan drama / Laura K. Egendorf, book editor.
        p.   cm. — (The Greenhaven Press companion to
    literary movements and genres)
    Includes bibliographical references and index.
    ISBN 0-7377-0205-2 (lib. bdg. : alk. paper) —
ISBN 0-7377-0204-4 (pbk. : alk. paper)
    1. English drama—Early modern and Elizabethan,
    1500–1600—History and criticism. 2. Shakespeare,
    William, 1564–1616—Criticism and interpretation.
    I. Egendorf, Laura K., 1973–   . II. Series.

PR653 .E643   2000
822'.309—dc21   99-055871
                                                         CIP

Cover photo: SuperStock

No part of this book may be reproduced or used in any form or by any means, electrical, mechanical, or otherwise, including, but not limited to, photocopy, recording, or any information storage and retrieval system, without prior written permission from the publisher.

Copyright ©2000 by Greenhaven Press, Inc.
PO Box 289009
San Diego, CA 92198-9009
Printed in the U.S.A.

CONTENTS

Chapter 1: The Characteristics of Elizabethan Drama

Chapter 2: Elizabethan Drama as a Reflection of Elizabethan Society

Chapter 3: An Examination of William Shakespeare

FOREWORD

The study of literature most often involves focusing on an individual work and uncovering its themes, stylistic conventions, and historical relevance. It is also enlightening to examine multiple works by a single author, identifying similarities and differences among texts and tracing the author's development as an artist.

While the study of individual works and authors is instructive, however, examining groups of authors who shared certain cultural or historical experiences adds a further richness to the study of literature. By focusing on literary movements and genres, readers gain a greater appreciation of influence of historical events and social circumstances on the development of particular literary forms and themes. For example, in the early twentieth century, rapid technological and industrial advances, mass urban migration, World War I, and other events contributed to the emergence of a movement known as American modernism. The dramatic social changes, and the uncertainty they created, were reflected in an increased use of free verse in poetry, the stream-of-consciousness technique in fiction, and a general sense of historical discontinuity and crisis of faith in most of the literature of the era. By focusing on these commonalities, readers attain a more comprehensive picture of the complex interplay of social, economic, political, aesthetic, and philosophical forces and ideas that create the tenor of any era. In the nineteenth-century American romanticism movement, for example, authors shared many ideas concerning the preeminence of the self-reliant individual, the infusion of nature with spiritual significance, and the potential of persons to achieve transcendence via communion with nature. However, despite their commonalities, American romantics often differed significantly in their thematic and stylistic approaches. Walt Whitman celebrated the communal nature of America's open democratic society, while Ralph Waldo

Emerson expressed the need for individuals to pursue their own fulfillment regardless of their fellow citizens. Herman Melville wrote novels in a largely naturalistic style whereas Nathaniel Hawthorne's novels were gothic and allegorical.

Another valuable reason to investigate literary movements and genres lies in their potential to clarify the process of literary evolution. By examining groups of authors, literary trends across time become evident. The reader learns, for instance, how English romanticism was transformed as it crossed the Atlantic to America. The poetry of Lord Byron, William Wordsworth, and John Keats celebrated the restorative potential of rural scenes. The American romantics, writing later in the century, shared their English counterparts' faith in nature; but American authors were more likely to present an ambiguous view of nature as a source of liberation as well as the dwelling place of personal demons. The whale in Melville's *Moby-Dick* and the forests in Hawthorne's novels and stories bear little resemblance to the benign pastoral scenes in Wordsworth's lyric poems.

Each volume in Greenhaven Press's Companions to Literary Movements and Genres series begins with an introductory essay that places the topic in a historical and literary context. The essays that follow are carefully chosen and edited for ease of comprehension. These essays are arranged into clearly defined chapters that are outlined in a concise annotated table of contents. Finally, a thorough chronology maps out crucial literary milestones of the movement or genre as well as significant social and historical events. Readers will benefit from the structure and coherence that these features lend to material that is often challenging. With Greenhaven's Literary Movements and Genres in hand, readers will be better able to comprehend and appreciate the major literary works and their impact on society.

Introduction

The First Folio, a collection of William Shakespeare's plays that was first published in 1623 (seven years after Shakespeare's death and shortly after the death of his wife), includes a poem written by Ben Jonson, a renowned dramatist in his own right and a contemporary of the Bard. Jonson praises Shakespeare's legacy and talents, declaring:

> Soule of the age!
> The applause! delight! the wonder of our stage!
> My *Shakespeare*, rise; I will not lodge thee by
> *Chaucer*, or *Spenser*, or bid *Beaumont* lye
> A little further, to make thee a roome:
> Thou art a Moniment, without a tombe,
> And art alive still, while thy Booke doth live,
> And we have wits to read, and praise to give.

Those words remain relevant. For of all the great literature that arose from the Elizabethan age, it is the work of William Shakespeare that makes a familiarity with Elizabethan drama essential. His work has influenced authors and artists for nearly four hundred years. If a reader does not understand Shakespeare, critics have argued, he or she is unlikely to truly understand literature.

Praise for Shakespeare's legacy and his role in the history of arts and literature is nearly universal. Sanford Pinsker, a professor of humanities at Franklin and Marshall College, notes that Shakespeare has long been considered "English literature's defining genius, the figure whose influence shaped—whether by imitation or opposition—the work of subsequent writers worth paying attention to."[1] Certain Shakespearean plays, such as *Hamlet*, are especially significant. In his book *The Ghosts of Hamlet: The Play and Modern Writers*, Martin Scofield examined the ways in which the tale of the Danish prince influenced writers as diverse as T.S. Eliot, James Joyce, and Søren Kierkegaard. Shakespeare's plays have also inspired a variety of composers, from Ludwig van Beethoven to Leonard Bernstein.

Shakespeare may be the most famous of Elizabethan dramatists, but a few of his contemporaries have also left their mark on arts and literature. Christopher Marlowe's play *Doctor Faustus*—the story of a man who sells his soul to the devil—has remained a popular tale, reworked by Johann Wolfgang von Goethe and others. Marlowe's output may have made a greater impact, perhaps even rivaling that of Shakespeare, had his career and life not ended abruptly at age twenty-nine. Other playwrights, such as Thomas Kyd and Robert Greene, are more obscure but they are still important, because Elizabethan dramatists often borrowed themes, characters, and plots from each other. Some of Shakespeare's greatest plays, including *Henry V* and *The Merchant of Venice*, borrow liberally from other Elizabethan playwrights and historians.

THE RELATIONSHIP BETWEEN DRAMA AND SOCIETY

Elizabethan dramatists were inspired not just by each other (as well as by ancient and medieval drama) but by the society in which they lived. The first great Elizabethan plays were written in the 1580s, paralleling the rise of England under Queen Elizabeth. During that decade, England transformed itself from a second-rank island off the coast of Europe into one of the world's great powers. But Britain's eminence did not guarantee its enlightenment. For example, because Africa was so remote from England's insular world, black Africans were subject to all sorts of spurious racism. Likewise, Jews who had been deemed greedy and conniving in popular (i.e., Christian) circles could not escape pernicious stereotyping. Shakespeare's *Othello* and *The Merchant of Venice* and Marlowe's *The Jew of Malta* acknowledged or even catered to those prejudices. Yet some of these works, such as Shakespeare's sympathetic portrayal of Othello, a black Moor, caused Elizabethans to reevaluate their assumptions, and thus stand both within and apart from their time.

Elizabethan drama is timeless not only because its plays did not merely parrot the majority views of the society, but also because the themes contained within the plays remain universal. Plays that depict the lives of doomed lovers, or the fate of men who seek too much power, have long been written. Nonetheless, it is *Romeo and Juliet*, *Macbeth*, and *Doctor Faustus* that continue to enchant and inspire. The plays may have been the product of a unique era, but they have stood the test of time. Society has changed since the days of Shake-speare, but the inner workings of people and their emotions and relationships remain much as they ever were, allowing these plays to retain their impact. The numerous film and stage adaptations of Shakespeare's plays are further proof that Elizabethan drama, particularly the plays of its most famous writer, continues to be relevant to the modern audience.

This volume examines the characteristics and key themes of the plays and assesses the importance of Elizabethan drama. By providing a wide range of views by some of the most renowned scholars of Elizabethan literature, the editor hopes that the modern reader will gain a greater awareness as to why so many of these plays have remained central to the development of arts and literature.

NOTE

1. Sanford Pinsker, "Why Shakespeare Is a Hard Sell in English Departments," *The World & I*, May 1997, p. 325.

A Historical Overview
of Elizabethan Drama

Few monarchs have made as great an impact on their kingdom and on the world as Elizabeth I of England. Her influence was so great that her reign, from 1558 to 1603, is known simply as the Elizabethan age. The queen was a powerful figurehead with considerable public and political support. After returning England to Protestantism following the Catholic reign of her half-sister, Mary I, Elizabeth quelled internal turmoil and unified her nation. And with a profound sense of nationalism, the British accomplished a great deal during Elizabeth's reign. Sir Francis Drake sailed around the world, the English navy defeated the mighty Spanish Armada, and England began to colonize the New World. By the time of Elizabeth's death, England had been transformed from a second-rank nation into one of the most powerful countries in all of Europe. Yet one of the most notable achievements of the Elizabethan age had little to do with political machinations or the success of the British navy. The literary achievement of the era, particularly drama, is striking. The works of playwrights including Ben Jonson, Christopher Marlowe, and most enduringly William Shakespeare delighted their contemporary audiences, influenced fellow and future writers, and have retained their stature for more than four centuries.

ANCIENT INFLUENCES

Although the Elizabethan dramas are often considered a product of their age, these plays were the result of an array of earlier literary influences. The development and growth of Elizabethan drama can be understood by examining these influences and by considering the ways that England under Elizabeth and the Elizabethan plays grew along parallel paths.

Prior to Elizabethan drama, the torch of Western drama was held aloft by its progenitors, the ancient Greeks and

Romans. Dramatists such as the Greek Menander and the Romans Seneca, Plautus, and Terence are considered to have greatly influenced Shakespeare and his contemporaries. From Menander, the Elizabethans learned the characteristics of New Comedy. As literary scholar Northrop Frye explains, the theme of New Comedy is "the successful effort of a young man to outwit an opponent and possess the girl of his choice."[1] One play that exhibits the qualities of New Comedy is Shakespeare's *The Two Gentlemen of Verona.* Plautus and Terence carried on the Menandrian tradition and further influenced Elizabethan dramatists by providing plot inspiration. One well-known example is Shakespeare's tale of reunited twins and mistaken identity, *The Comedy of Errors,* which fuses the Plautus plays *Meneachmi* and *Amphitruo.* Elizabethans also borrowed the Terentian double-plot structure, which originally featured two tightly unified storylines; but, as Richard Hosley notes in his critique, "The Formal Influence of Plautus and Terence," the Elizabethan double plots were not as tightly integrated. Hosley explains how the Elizabethan double plot evolved from the Terentian plays:

> Normally the two separate actions [of Elizabethan plays] are more distinct in respect of atmosphere, characterisation, theme and conduct of the action than the two plots of a Terentian double-plot play; and we sometimes acknowledge their loose integration by calling them *parallel* actions. Probably the development of the tightly-knit double-action play of Terence into the more loosely-knit double-action play of Elizabethan comedy (and tragedy) is to be attributed in part to the work of [John] Lyly and [Robert] Greene but chiefly to Shakespeare's achievements in such plays as *The Taming of the Shrew, The Merchant of Venice, Much Ado About Nothing,* and *Twelfth Night.*[2]

While echoes of Menander, Plautus, and Terence can be heard in Elizabethan comedy, it is the classical plays of Seneca that had the most influence on Elizabethan tragedy. Accessible sixteenth-century translations of Seneca's works were popular among the English. Although some critics argue that Seneca's impact has been overstated, other scholars contend that were it not for *Hercules Furens, Thyestes,* and other Senecan plays, tragedies such as Shakespeare's *Macbeth* and Thomas Kyd's *The Spanish Tragedy* might not have been penned. Senecan traits such as horrific violence, supernatural elements, and the theme of revenge are present in these and other Elizabethan plays.

THE IMPACT OF MEDIEVAL DRAMAS

More than a millennium passed before the arrival of the next great influence on Elizabethan drama: the medieval miracle plays, morality plays, and interludes. Miracle plays were performed throughout Europe as early as the thirteenth century. Their anonymous authors dealt chiefly with religious stories: anecdotes from the Bible or depictions of saintly lives. Miracle plays were also known as mysteries, from the Latin word *ministerium*, which means "act." On Corpus Christi and other feast days, residents of English towns such as Wakefield and Chester gathered along the streets to watch a cycle of miracle plays performed in its entirety, depicting biblical history from the Creation to Judgment Day.

Miracle plays evolved into moralities. These dramas also contained religious and moral themes but employed allegory rather than biblical stories to convey their message. In one of the most famous moralities, *Everyman*, the title character faces Death and meets other allegorical characters, including Good Deeds and Knowledge, as he prepares for his journey to the afterlife. The play concludes with the soul of Everyman departing for heaven. While these plays are generally considered not as skillfully written as the Elizabethan works, Glynne Wickham, in his book *Shakespeare's Dramatic Heritage: Collected Studies in Mediaeval, Tudor and Shakespearean Drama*, contends that the moralities laid the groundwork for the later plays:

> I hope . . . to make one general point about the dramatic qualities of the Morality Play acceptable: the wide-ranging nature of the narrative and plot material that was allowable within the genre. I believe this to have been one of its greatest strengths: for it enabled the authors and the actors to develop their crafts experimentally little by little, while depending for their broad effects upon well-tried routines with which their audiences were already familiar. These are the conditions which pave the way to virtuosity in any art. They are the conditions with which, a century later, William Shakespeare and Richard Burbage were to be confronted as members of the Lord Chamberlain's and King's Companies at the Globe.[5]

The next step in the ladder of influences on Elizabethan drama was the advent of interludes. Typically a dialogue between two or more persons, these plays were often performed during a break in a royal or noble banquet. Interludes began as shorter morality plays but gradually became increasingly secular and comedic. John Heywood wrote some of the most memorable interludes, including *Johan the Husband* and *The Four P's.* By shying away from religious themes, the interludes made it acceptable for the later Elizabethan dramatists to write plays that had little, if anything, to do with the Bible.

THE BEGINNING OF ELIZABETHAN DRAMA

All the aforementioned influences informed the development of Tudor—and more specifically Elizabethan—drama. Tudor drama spanned the reigns of Henry VIII and his children Edward, Mary, and Elizabeth. Nicholas Udall's comedy *Ralph Roister Doister*, initially performed in the 1540s, is one of the more famous examples of pre-Elizabethan Tudor drama. These early plays were typically more farcical than their successors and featured characters from the lower and middle classes. While the Tudor dramas did share some characteristics with Elizabethan dramas, such as Roman and Greek influences and largely secular plots, the playwrights were not as skilled as those who followed. The earliest plays of the narrower Elizabethan era were produced not long after Elizabeth ascended the throne in 1558. *Gammer Garton's Needle* (author unknown) is considered one of the earliest Elizabethan comedies, performed in the 1560s. And in 1565, Thomas Sackville and Thomas Norton published *Gorboduc*, the first Senecan-tinged Elizabethan tragedy. *Gorboduc* is also important because of its use of language, notes John Addington Symonds in *Shakspere's Predecessors in the English Drama*: "It is . . . the first play written in Blank Verse.[4] . . . Norton and Sackville brought it into dramatic literature—tame as yet in cadence and monotonous in structure; but with so fateful and august a future, that this humble cradle of its birth commands our reverence."[5]

These early Elizabethan plays are considered inferior in writing quality and character development to those that followed. It was not until the 1580s that Elizabethan drama flowered, mirroring the time when Elizabeth's reign reached its greatest heights. The era and the drama grew alongside one another. That decade, which marked the midpoint of Elizabeth's reign, saw the queen and her country firmly established as a major world power. The execution of Mary, Queen of Scots, in 1587, at the behest of the Elizabethan court, eliminated the greatest internal challenge to Elizabeth's throne. England demonstrated its political and naval strength by defeating the Spanish Armada in 1588, and thus dashing Catholic Europe's hopes of suppressing the Protestant upstarts.

THE UNIVERSITY WITS

It was around that time that the first true Elizabethan dramatists—John Lyly, Robert Greene, and Marlowe, among others—emerged. These men, university graduates in their twenties and thirties, have been dubbed the University Wits. Their plays, which featured blank verse and often examined the ways in which an outsider can usurp power through treachery (shades of Niccolo Machiavelli's *The Prince*), rang the death knell for the moralities. The greatest of the Wits was arguably Christopher Marlowe. He was born into a middle-class family in 1564, the son of a shoemaker who later became a church warden. In 1581 Marlowe earned a scholarship to Corpus Christi College at Cambridge University and received a bachelor's and master's degree. His life and career, however, were brief. He died in a tavern fight in 1593, leaving only a handful of plays and poems, including the drama *Tamburlaine the Great, Parts I and II*, which according to literary scholar G.K. Hunter best exemplifies the goal of the Wits. "Here at last we have a work of popular entertainment which openly claims classic status, whose presence visibly altered the landscape in which it appeared and charged its environment with new meanings."[6] Despite Marlowe's influential creations, and other plays by his compatriots—John Lyly's *Endimion*, George Peele's *Locrine*, and Robert Greene's *Pandosto*, among others—the University Wits did not radically change English theater. The University Wits despised the popular theater and sought to use their education to write more erudite drama appealing to intellectuals and elites. They did not achieve their goal because Elizabethan popular culture expected the Wits to hew to certain traditional dramatic forms, so Marlowe and his peers sacrificed artistic ideals to survive as popular playwrights. According to Hunter:

> The University Wits sought to change the conditions of playwriting, for good authorial reasons; they sought to redefine it as an activity that would allow them to impose their literary values on the extant institutions. In such matters, however, individuals may propose, but institutions dispose. And insti-

tutions seldom accept change unless there are good institutional reasons for doing so (decline in profits, problems of public order, trouble with censorship).[7]

THE COMING OF WILLIAM SHAKESPEARE

Ironically, it was a man with a grammar-school education who succeeded where the University Wits had failed. William Shakespeare, whose career lasted slightly more than two decades, produced thirty-eight plays and numerous poems that are widely considered not only the culmination of the era but masterpieces of world literature. Yet while his plays have spawned shelf upon shelf of critique and analysis, not much is known about the playwright himself.

At first glance, nothing in Shakespeare's life story would predict his creation of so many timeless comedies, tragedies, and histories. He was born in April 1564 (most likely on April 23, according to baptismal records) to John and Mary Shakespeare in Stratford-upon-Avon. Mary Shakespeare came from a wealthy family, and her dowry helped provide the Shakespeares with a degree of financial stability and improved social status. John Shakespeare made gloves, sold wool, and held various public offices, including high bailiff. John Shakespeare's accomplishments, which also included property ownership, gained his family some social mobility and enabled William Shakespeare and his brothers to attend grammar school, which presumably included the study of Greek and Roman classics. Shakespeare most likely concluded his schooling in his midteens. At age eighteen, Shakespeare wed the already-pregnant Anne Hathaway, with whom he would have three children (including his only son, Hamnet, who died at age eleven). Little is known about Shakespeare's life from 1583 to 1592. By the latter year, Shakespeare had moved to London alone and begun acting in and writing plays, starting with *1 Henry VI.* He died in 1616. In 1623, following the death of Anne, actors Henry Condell and John Heminge published his plays as a collection known as the First Folio.

THE AUTHORSHIP DEBATE

It is the relative simplicity of Shakespeare's life, in fact, that has made some people wonder whether he is the rightful author of the plays that bear his name. Some scholars have speculated that Christopher Marlowe did not die in that tavern brawl and lived to write the Shakespearean oeuvre. Others vigorously advance the theory that philosopher and statesman Francis Bacon is the true author of the plays. Perhaps the most promising contender is Edward de Vere, whose legitimacy is supported by a group known as the Oxfordians. Since 1920, Oxfordians have claimed that de Vere, the seventeenth earl of Oxford, hid behind the identity of the otherwise undistinguished actor William Shakspere[8] because many Elizabethan playwrights, particularly the nobility, sought anonymity. Oxfordians contend that the earl's life closely paralleled the stories in the plays. In contrast, they opine, it is unlikely that Shakspere, who was not known to have traveled to Italy and was not part of the Elizabethan court, could have written plays so full of detail about life among nobility or in Verona and Venice.

Stratfordians—those who support the authenticity of William Shakespeare—decry the Oxfordian thesis, suggesting in part that Oxfordians are classist in their assumption that Shakespeare, a man of middle-class origins, lacked the background and education needed to write the plays. Jonathan Bate, the author of *The Genius of Shakespeare*, wrote an article in 1999 for *Harper's* noting that Shakespeare was not the only grammar-school graduate who wrote memorable drama. "[Ben Jonson's plays] are vastly more academic than Shakespeare's, yet they, too, were written on the foundation of nothing more than a grammar-school education. The thing is, Elizabethan grammar schools were very good. They put our high schools to deep shame."[9]

WHY SHAKESPEARE'S PLAYS HAVE ENDURED

The debate over the authorship of Shakespeare's plays remains unresolved. What is irrefutable is that, unlike most of the works of his contemporaries, Shakespeare's plays have stood the test of time. Playhouses the world over mount productions of *As You Like It* and *Othello*; a person who has never read a word of Shakespeare can still recognize lines of dialogue from *Hamlet* that have entered common usage. Film versions of the plays proliferate, ranging from adaptations that retain every word of Shakespeare's dialogue to modern reworkings of the plots of *The Taming of the Shrew*, *Romeo and Juliet*, and *Richard III*.

Literary scholars and critics advance a variety of theories to explain why Shakespeare is the greatest of Elizabethan dramatists. According to Margaret Webster, in her contribution to *The Living Shakespeare*, the ascendancy of England in the 1580s inspired Shakespeare: "It may be fairly said, I think, that Shakespeare was born at the full tide of England's history and that his genius matched the richness of the hour. Perhaps at no other time, before or since, could it have reached such stature. The very air crackled with vitality, with challenge and change."[10] According to Harold Bloom, Shakespeare is great because his plays are universal, able to be read and appreciated by most people. "If any author has become a mortal god, it must be Shakespeare. Who can dispute his good eminence, to which merit alone raised him? . . . Common readers, and thankfully we still possess them, rarely can read Dante; yet they can read and attend Shakespeare."[11]

However, Shakespeare did not stand wholly apart from his contemporaries or his predecessors. He borrowed many plots and characters from earlier works. Raphael Holinshed's *Chronicles*, first published in 1577, was a key source for the history plays, *Macbeth*, and *King Lear*. Other plays such as *The Taming of the Shrew*, *Othello*, and *Romeo and Juliet* were adapted from English and European sources. Contemporaries, particularly Kyd and Marlowe, helped shape Shakespeare's writing style and approach to characters. Without Barabas, the title character in Marlowe's *The Jew of Malta*, Shakespeare may never have devised Aaron from *Titus Andronicus* or Shylock from *The Merchant of Venice*. But Shakespeare was not the only heavy borrower among the Elizabethan dramatists; certain sources, including Roman historian Livy's tale of Appius and Virginia and the medieval King Arthur legends, were mined for a plethora of plays.

However, even when mining older material, Shakespeare remained head and shoulders above his peers. Although his contemporaries such as Kyd and Marlowe imported the techniques of the revenge tragedies, Shakespeare's adaptations of older styles were always improved by his use of characters of greater depth. Ostensibly *Hamlet* is a revenge play, but Shakespeare has created such a complex title character that the act of revenge pales next to Hamlet's musings on madness, responsibility, and the nature of existence. Thus, Shakespeare's works reach beyond common plots and provide thoughtful insights on timeless themes. Recognizing this quality in Shakespeare's plays, Symonds writes:

The forms he employs are the forms he found in common usage among his fellow-craftsmen. But his method of employing them is so vastly superior, the quality of his work is so incommensurable by any standard we apply to the best of theirs, that we cannot help regarding the plays of Shakspere as not exactly different in kind, but diverse in inspiration.[12]

UNDERSTANDING THE ELIZABETHAN THEATER

However, Elizabethan drama is not just words on a page, waiting for a literary dissection. Elizabethan drama is meant to be performed, not merely read. Many of the playwrights, including Shakespeare and Jonson, also acted in their own plays and those of others. Shakespeare is believed to have played Adam in *As You Like It* and the Ghost in *Hamlet*; he also acted in Jonson's *Every Man in His Humour.*

Unlike modern times, when Shakespeare's plays are often considered high culture, the Elizabethans considered the theater to be essentially pop culture—the plays were the movies and television of the sixteenth century. The poorest families may have rarely been able to attend plays, but the majority of townspeople could afford to visit the theater on occasion. Seating prices ranged from one penny for "groundlings," who stood in front of the stage, to two or three cents for gallery seats. A few wealthy patrons paid six cents to sit directly onstage. Although not everyone approved of their presence, women, including the queen herself, sometimes attended the theater. Elizabeth's great love of the theater was an essential factor in the growth of drama, because civic and religious leaders in London considered plays sinful. Symonds writes: "Though the social influence of plays on the youth of London was at least questionable, neither the last Tudor nor the first Stuart attempted to suppress them on this account. Besides enjoying theatrical representations with key relish herself, Elizabeth seems to have understood their utility as a means of popular education."[13]

As for the theater itself, the typical structure of the Elizabethan playhouse was an open-air arena. Plays were performed in the afternoon so as to utilize natural light. Private indoor theaters, such as Blackfriars, did use candles for illumination, but those theaters were designed for smaller, wealthier audiences. The stage included a central platform divided by columns, a trapdoor, an alcove, a balcony, and sometimes a level above the balcony. These various spaces allowed several actions to occur onstage simultaneously. Although the stage structure was complex, it was largely devoid of props and scenery. Audiences were alerted to changes in setting by placards or dialogue.

The structural complexity of the Elizabethan stage echoes the complexity of the plays, which featured a variety of themes that appealed to audiences. History plays depicted the triumphs and tragedies of the monarchs who preceded Elizabeth. Biases were evident in certain histories, particularly Shakespeare's *Richard III.* Richard was slain by the earl of Richmond, who as Henry VII established the Tudor line that ended with Elizabeth, so it was understandable that Shakespeare would seek to glorify the Tudors by portraying Richard III as an unscrupulous monarch crippled with a hunched back. Though historian Thomas More first established Richard as a hunchbacked villain, it was Shakespeare who made that image indelible in the eyes of thousands of theatergoers. According to Herschel Baker in his introduction to *Richard III* in *The Riverside Shakespeare*: "[More's] *The History of King Richard the Third* must be accounted one of the most persistent triumphs in English historical literature, for thanks to Shakespeare's use of it—and despite modern efforts to salvage Richard's reputation—it has lasted to this day."[14] On the other hand, Henry V, a more popular king, is depicted as a hero, even though his actual behavior was far different from Shakespeare's portrayal. Nineteenth-century literary critic William Hazlitt comments on the differences between Henry V's historical and literary character:

> Henry V it is true, was a hero, a King of England, and the conqueror of the king of France. Yet we feel little love or admiration for him. He was a hero, that is, he was ready to sacrifice his own life for the pleasure of destroying thousands of other lives: he was a king of England, but not a constitutional one, and we only like kings according to the law; lastly, he was a conqueror of the French king, and for this we dislike him less than if he had conquered the French people. How then do we like him? We like him in the play. There he is a very amiable monster, a very splendid pageant.[15]

SOCIAL BIASES IN ELIZABETHAN DRAMA

While the portrayal of monarchs in the history plays reflected those kings' popularity, plot and characterization in the comedies and tragedies reflected the prejudices of the Elizabethan audience. The Elizabethan treatment of Jews and blacks informed several of its dramas. The anti-Semitism of the Elizabeth era can be seen in a variety of plays, most notably *The Jew of Malta* and *The Merchant of Venice*, that feature villainous Jews. Barabas and Shylock place their mercenary desires above everything else, but the Christian audience sees the two Jews get their comeuppance—Barabas falls into a vat of boiling oil, while Shylock is required to convert to Christianity. Africans were another non-Christian population that fascinated and frightened the Elizabethans. Shakespeare's depiction of the African soldier Othello, one of his greatest creations, both reflects and explodes the Elizabethan stereotypes. Some of the European characters in *Othello* describe the Moor in stereotypical terms, labeling him a violent savage and sexual predator. However, when Othello meets a tragic end, it is not because he is barbaric. The Moor is a courageous soldier with a noble mien, and Shakespeare goes against Elizabethan biases by having the typical human failings of jealousy and distrust lead to Othello's fall.

It is in the presentation of women in Elizabethan drama, however, that the intersection between the society and its plays is most clear. Ironically, there could be no wholly realistic representation of women in the plays, because women were not allowed on the Elizabeth stage. Instead, boys played the female roles. This ban on female actors was just one restriction on the lives of Elizabethan women, restrictions that were shown in many of the plays. According to Elizabethan mores even the best-educated and wealthiest women—with the notable exception of the queen—needed the protection of a husband and family. No matter how witty or resourceful or spirited a woman might be—a Rosalind in *As You Like It* or Kate in *The Taming of the Shrew*—her only respectable future role was that of wife. The Protestant Reformation ostensibly increased the rights and responsibilities of women, although professor and author Lisa Jardine suggests that the Reformation in fact reduced female independence:

> Two direct consequences of Protestant reform had the accidental effect of disadvantaging women and women's thought. The abolition of the convents removed a sphere of separatist, independent activity for women. . . . And the abolition of saint worship . . . removed a moral support from women.[16]

As the Puritans gained influence in the late sixteenth century, women did begin to gain a measure of dignity and independence in marriage that was heretofore unknown. The plays showed this slow evolution of marriage, with Desdemona and Emilia of *Othello* and other ill-treated wives depicted as more noble and virtuous than their husbands.

THE END OF ELIZABETHAN DRAMA

Queen Elizabeth had privileges and powers unavailable to other Elizabethan women, but immortality was not one of them. Her death in 1603 ended the reign of the Tudors, as her successor, James I, established the Stuart line. Nonetheless, though Elizabeth was no longer a physical presence in the theater, she remained an influence on drama long after her death. Hence, just as Elizabethan drama did not truly begin until well into her reign, neither did it end at her death. No true end to Elizabethan drama—or beginning of Jacobean drama (for James I), for that matter—has been universally established. Possible ending dates range from the queen's death through the middle of the seventeenth century, when the nation was embroiled in civil war between Charles II and Parliament. Some scholars might label *The White Devil* (ca. 1612) by John Webster an Elizabethan tragedy; others call it Jacobean. *Macbeth* is in part a flattery of James, England's Scottish-born monarch, but its Senecan elements also mark it as Elizabethan. As the beginning and ending dates of Elizabethan drama appear to be a matter of interpretation, perhaps it can be suggested that this epoch ended on the death of Shakespeare, its greatest creator.

Yet even now, nearly four centuries after the deaths of its namesake and its most esteemed playwright, Elizabethan drama has not truly died. Shakespeare's plays continue to be performed on stage, film, and television. Characters such as Hamlet and Othello are part of not only the Western cultural heritage but the Eastern as well. Japanese director Akira Kurosawa's *Throne of Blood*, for example, is his reinterpretation of *Macbeth*. Shakespeare's plays have also inspired a host of musical compositions and operas, from Giuseppe Verdi's *Otello* to Peter Tchaikovsky's *Romeo and Juliet* to Leonard Bernstein's *West Side Story*. The Elizabethan era also pervades the language of the average person. Shakespeare invented a host of common words and phrases, such as "fair play," "lonely," and "catch cold."

The plays written by Shakespeare, Marlowe, and the other Elizabethan dramatists were just one triumph of the Elizabethan age. Just as England gained wealth, power, and stability under Elizabeth's reign, so too did the drama move from weak and unvaried imitations of earlier forms to a new form that, while influenced by its predecessors, took on characteristics that made it unique and memorable. With the exception of scholars and students of literature and history, society has largely forgotten the miracle plays and moralities, and the kings and queens who ruled while they were performed; the accomplishments of the Elizabethan age and the drama that bears its name endure. As educator and scholar Felix E. Schelling explains, "[The English drama] grew to be the peculiar art in which the worldly and vigorous yet ideal and poetical age of Elizabeth found its most lasting and characteristic expression."[17]

NOTES

1. Northrop Frye, "The Argument of Comedy," in D.A. Robertson Jr., ed., *English Institute Essays 1948*. New York: Columbia University Press, 1949, p. 58.

2. Richard Hosley, "The Formal Influence of Plautus and Terence," in John Russell Brown and Bernard Harris, eds., *Stratford-Upon-Avon Studies 9: Elizabethan Theatre*. New York: St. Martin's Press, 1967, p. 133.

3. Glynne Wickham, *Shakespeare's Dramatic Heritage: Collected Studies in Mediaeval, Tudor and Shakespearean Drama*. New York: Barnes & Noble, 1969, pp. 29–30.

4. Blank verse is unrhymed verse, often in iambic pentameter.

5. John Addington Symonds, *Shakspere's Predecessors in the English Drama*. London: Smith, Elder, 1904, p. 189.

6. G.K. Hunter, "The Beginnings of Elizabethan Drama: Revolution and Continuity," in Mary Beth Rose, ed., *Renaissance Drama, New Series XVII: Renaissance Drama and Cultural Change*. Evanston, IL: Northwestern University Press, 1986, p. 35.

7. G.K. Hunter, "The Beginnings of Elizabethan Drama," p. 48.

8. Spelling was not consistent in the sixteenth century, so several variations on Shakespeare's name exist. Shakspere is the spelling preferred, though not exclusively, by Oxfordians, who use this spelling to refer to whom they consider to be the historically unimportant man who was born in Stratford-upon-Avon.

9. Jonathan Bate, "Golden Lads and Chimney-Sweepers," *Harper's Magazine*, April 1999, p. 61.

10. Margaret Webster, "Shakespeare in His Time," in Robert Gittings, ed., *The Living Shakespeare*. New York: Barnes & Noble, 1960, p. 12.

11. Harold Bloom, *Shakespeare: The Invention of the Human*. New York: Riverhead Books, 1998, p. 3.

12. Symonds, *Shakspere's Predecessors,* p. 14.

13. Symonds, *Shakspere's Predecessors,* p. 66.

14. Herschel Baker, Introduction to *Richard III,* in G. Blakemore Evans, ed., *The Riverside Shakespeare.* Boston: Houghton Mifflin, 1974, pp. 708–709.

15. William Hazlitt, *Characters of Shakespear's Plays.* 2nd ed. London: Taylor & Hessey, 1818. Quoted in William Shakespeare, *The Life of Henry V,* ed. John Russell Brown. New York: Penguin Books, 1988, pp. 212–13.

16. Lisa Jardine, *Still Harping on Daughters: Women and Drama in the Age of Shakespeare.* New York: Columbia University Press, 1989, p. 50.

17. Felix E. Schelling, *Elizabethan Drama, 1558–1642.* Vol. 1. New York: Russell & Russell, 1959.

CHAPTER 1

The Characteristics of Elizabethan Drama

Elizabethan
Drama

Elizabethan Drama Reflects the Atmosphere of the English Renaissance

John Addington Symonds

The English Renaissance of the sixteenth and seventeenth centuries is the result of two major intellectual influences: the Italian Renaissance and the German Reformation. John Addington Symonds argues that the intellectual atmosphere of the English Renaissance finds its artistic voice in the romantic drama. According to Symonds, the chief characteristics of English romantic drama are spontaneity and freedom, a reflection on the society from which it springs. Such freedom is shown by British playwrights' rejection of traditional Latin or Italian dramatic structure, opting instead for a greater use of dialogue and a mixing of tragic and comic elements, which differed from the unity of tone sought by earlier dramatists. Symonds was a nineteenth-century poet, writer, and art historian.

In the short space of this . . . essay, I cannot attempt to sketch the history of the drama, or to criticize the various schools of style which were formed in the course of its passage from maturity to decadence. It must be enough for me to indicate in what way the genius of the English nation expressed itself through this form of art at the epoch when the Reformation had been accomplished, the attacks of Spain repulsed, and the new learning of the Renaissance assimilated.

England, alone of European nations, received the influences of both Renaissance and Reformation simultaneously. These two great movements of the modern intellect, which closed the Middle Ages, and opened a new period of mental

Excerpted from the Introduction, by John Addington Symonds, to *Christopher Marlowe*, edited by Havelock Ellis (London: Vizetelly, 1887).

culture for the Western nations, have to be regarded as distinct because their issues were different, and they were severally accomplished by Latin and Teutonic races. Yet both Renaissance and Reformation had a common starting point in humanism; both needed the revival of learning for their motive force; both effected a liberation of the spirit from authority, superstition and decadent ideals. . . .

The new learning, derived from the revival of antiquity, had already permeated Italian and French literature. Classical erudition had been adapted to the needs of modern thought; the chief Greek and Latin authors had been translated into modern languages; the masterpieces of antiquity were interpreted and made intelligible. English scholars, trained upon the new method by private tutors or in the now regenerated public schools, began at once to translate the poets and historians of antiquity and of Italy into the vernacular. . . .

[England was] in possession of all the materials for building up a mighty edifice of literary art. Little at this period had been accomplished in pure poetry. It is true that Sir Thomas Wyat, Henry Howard (Earl of Surrey) and Philip Sidney had acclimatized the sonnet; that blank verse had been introduced; and that Spenser was just giving his noble epic [*The Faerie Queene*] to the world. But the people in its youthful vigour under Tudor Sovereigns . . . needed some wider, some more comprehensive sphere for the display of its native genius; and this it found in the romantic drama, to which, notwithstanding the efforts of students and polite persons, it adhered with the pertinacity of instinct. This drama, its own original creation, stood to the English nation in the place of all the other arts. It became for [England] the embodiment of that Renaissance which had given sculpture, painting, architecture and a gorgeous undergrowth of highly-coloured poetry to the Italians. . . .

THE ENGLISH STAGE

Just as the Romantic Drama was a home-product of the English people, so the method of presenting plays in London, and the material conditions of the stage, were eminently homely. It had been customary during the Middle Ages to exhibit Miracles[1] upon wooden platforms or moveable waggons, which were set up in the marketplaces of towns, or on

1. plays that presented biblical stories or reenacted saints' lives

the turfed enclosures of abbatial buildings. Moralities[2] and Interludes[3] were shown publicly during civic entertainments, or privately at the request of companies assembled in some noble dwelling; a portion of the hall being devoted for the nonce [present purpose] to wandering actors. . . . Meanwhile, when secular dramas, intended for the delectation of the people at large, began to emerge from the Moralities, it became customary to use the yards of inns, bear-gardens,[4] and such places for their performance. This led by gradual degrees to the establishment of regular theatres, which, though they were violently opposed by the municipal authorities, and inveighed against from the pulpit, contrived to root themselves in the suburbs, along the further bank of the Thames, and in the fields toward Shoreditch. Even the best London theatres between the years 1580 and 1630 were simple wooden buildings, round or hexagonal in shape. The larger stood open to the air; the smaller were roofed in. The former had the name of public, the latter of private houses. Performances took place in the afternoon, usually at three o'clock. Scenery was almost wholly lacking: thus if Thebes or Verona had to be imagined by the audience, a sign-post bore the name of Thebes or Verona upon a tower of lath and plaster. The stage itself projected so far into the pit or yard, as it was called, that the actors were brought close to the spectators beneath and around them. Playgoers who could afford this luxury, were accommodated with stools upon the stage; others might take boxes or rooms, as they were then termed, just above the heads of the groundlings standing in the circular space of the yard. Prices varied from threepence for entrance only to about two shillings for the most expensive places in the best theatres. No actresses appeared upon the English boards, and all female parts were played by boys. It was also usual for the choristers of St. Paul's or of the Chapel Royal to perform whole dramas. Some of Ben Jonson's colossal Comedies were first given to the public by these "Children;" and I may remind students of William Shakespeare's *Hamlet* that the companies of adult actors regarded them as formidable competitors. In reading any masterpiece of the Elizabethan and Jacobean periods, these facts should never be forgotten. To the simplicity of the theatres,

---

2. an offshoot of miracle plays that used allegory to teach Christian morals and ethics   3. shorter plays, typically in dialogue, that developed from moralities but gradually involved more secular plots   4. arenas that were used for bearbaiting

the absence of scenical resources, and the close contact of the players with their audience, we may ascribe many peculiarities of our Romantic Drama—notably its disregard of the unities of time and place, and its eloquent appeals by descriptive passages to the imagination. Its marvellous fecundity in second-rate artistic work, hastily produced and readily neglected, may also be referred to similar circumstances.

These considerations explain the extraordinary force, variety, and imaginative splendour of the works poured forth with such prolific energy for the humble theatres of London during the fifty years which followed the great date of 1587.[5] It won a golden time, between the perils of the Armada[6] and the convulsions of the Great Rebellion,[7] just long enough to round and complete a monument of art representative of [England's] national life at its most brilliant period. In order to comprehend the English Renaissance, we must not be satisfied with studying only Shakespeare. We must learn to know his predecessors, contemporaries, and successors; that multitude of men inferior to him in stature, but of the same lineage; each of whom in greater or less degree was inspired with the like genius; each of whom possessed a clairvoyance into human nature and a power of presenting it vividly to the imagination which can be claimed by no similar group of fellow-workers in the history of any literature now known to us. What made the play-wrights of that epoch so great as to deserve the phrase which [English poet] John Dryden found for them—"Theirs was the giant race before the flood"—was that they lived and wrote in fullest sympathy with the whole people. The public to which they appealed was the English nation, from Elizabeth upon the throne down to the lowest ragamuffin of the streets. In the same wooden theatres met lords and ladies, citizens and prentices, sailors and working-men, pickpockets, country-folk, and captains from the wars. The men who wrote for this mixed audience were hampered by no cumbrous stage-

---

5. Mary Queen of Scots, who was next in line to the British throne after Elizabeth I, was executed in England in 1587 following an imprisonment of nearly 20 years. The Elizabethan court considered Mary a threat because of the plots devised by Mary and her Catholic supporters to overthrow Elizabeth. Mary's death led to greater conflict between Catholic Spain and Protestant England. While Mary never became Queen of England, her son James succeeded Elizabeth in 1603.   6. The Armada was a Spanish fleet of ships sent by King Philip II in 1588 to invade England. The English navy's victory over the Armada helped establish England as a major power.   7. A civil war waged between supporters of King Charles I and supporters of the Parliament and Parliamentarian general Oliver Cromwell. It lasted from 1642 to 1651 and included the execution of Charles in 1649.

properties, by no crushing gorgeousness of scenery, by no academical propriety, by no courtly etiquette, by no interference from agents of police or spies of a jealous hierarchy. So long as they preserved decorum in the elementary decencies of morals and religion, their hands were free; and they had the whole spirit of a vividly alive and warmly interested race to stimulate their genius. It is not to be wondered in these circumstances that men of minor talents rose above their mediocrity; that sturdy giants like Jonson grew to Titans; or that a John Webster and a John Fletcher climbed the clouds at times and took their seat among the gods.

THE TRAITS OF ROMANTIC DRAMA

If we now ask what is the distinctive mark of this Drama, we may answer in two words: spontaneity and freedom. It has the spontaneity of an art-product indigenous and native to [England's] soil, though all the culture of the Classics and the Renaissance contributed to make it wealthy. It has the freedom of a great race conscious of their adolescent vigour, the freedom of combatants victorious in a struggle only less momentous than that of Hellas [Greece] against Persia, the freedom of a land bounded upon all sides by the ocean, the freedom of high-spirited men devoted to a mistress [Queen Elizabeth] who personified for them the power and majesty of Britain. Its freedom is freedom from pedantry, from servility to scholastic rules, from observance of foreign or antiquated models; freedom from the dread of political or ecclesiastical oppression; freedom from courtly obsequiousness and class-prejudices. In use of language, moulding of character, copying of manners, and treatment of dramatic themes, no less than in the minor technicalities of versification, each writer stamps a recognizable mint-mark on his own work, without regard to precedent or what the lettered world will think of him. Critics who appreciate the niceties and proprieties which can to some extent be secured by Academical supervision, may complain that the English Drama suffered from this spontaneity and freedom—that it would have attained to fairer proportions if the playwrights had aimed more at correctness, and that posterity could have foregone seven-tenths of their performances if the remaining three-tenths had exhibited maturer art and more patient execution. To deny an underlying truth in this criticism, would be idle. We are bound to acknowledge that the fine

qualities of spontaneity and freedom, here displayed so liberally, have their corresponding faults of carelessness, incompleteness, and indifference to form. The masterpieces of
our Romantic Drama, when the majority of Shakespeare's
plays have been excepted, are few in number. . . . Yet it remains true that even the rank jungle of mediocre work surviving from that epoch is permeated with the same life and
freshness, the same juvenile audacity, the same frank touch
on nature, the same keen insight into human motives and
emotions, as those rarer pieces of accomplished art which
deserve to be classed with the monuments of Attic tragedy. It
is this stupendous mass of plays, evolved upon the same
lines and vivified by one national spirit, which makes [En-
gland's] Drama unique. The spontaneity and freedom, again,
of which I have been speaking, form so conspicuous a note
of Elizabethan literature that when the genius of our race
and language takes a new direction under conditions
favourable to liberty, . . . poets turn their eyes instinctively to
the old dramatists, assimilate their audacities, and do not
shun their imperfections.

Elizabethan Drama Exhibits Medieval Influences

John Wasson

John Wasson maintains that while the influence of morality plays on Elizabethan drama is not as great as some scholars have suggested, three types of medieval plays did help shape the characteristics of English drama. Medieval folk plays and Renaissance comedy feature a pattern of potential disaster followed by redemption. The miracle plays, which depict the lives of saints, also helped shape Elizabethan historical dramas. *Henry IV* and other histories borrow medieval techniques found in miracle plays, including rearranging historical events, using anachronisms, and writing a subplot that parallels the main plot. Although none of the texts survive, the most likely medieval influence on Elizabethan tragedy is the Thomas à Becket plays, written from 1182 until the reign of Henry VIII. The Becket plays depict the fate of a man who makes a moral choice and faces the ensuing consequences. These three types of medieval plays show that Elizabethan drama is a natural descendent of the theater that preceded it. Wasson is a writer of several books on English drama and has taught at Washington State University.

Part of the problem in our obtaining a clear perspective on the development of English drama is that we have, understandably, based our judgments on extant texts. David Bevington, in *From Mankind to Marlowe,* was led to base his conclusions upon plays "offered for acting" on the assumption that casting patterns published with them provided a "prima-facie inference" that they "were intended for the professional market." But those plays seem mostly to have been

Excerpted from "The Morality Play: Ancestor of Elizabethan Drama?" by John Wasson, *Comparative Drama,* Fall 1979. Reprinted by permission of the editors of *Comparative Drama.*

written by courtiers and schoolmasters, not the usual writers of plays for professional companies. In any case, one sus-
pects that the plays were "offered for acting" by schoolboys;
there would have been no profit in the few copies small professional troupes might purchase, but considerable profit if
a hundred grammar schools decided to produce a particular
play. Unlike the school plays, early professional plays, not
being considered "art" and having no selling power by the
names or prestige of their authors, were probably seldom
printed. Later professional plays were printed for a new
reading public, but not for the use of rival troupes. In short,
the extant early Tudor interludes[1] may not have been at all
typical of the plays being acted by professionals, though they
may still tell us much. . . . Even more clearly, it now appears
that of all the drama acted before 1500, it was the unusual,
not the normal, which was preserved. For example, almost
the only English mystery plays[2] we have are those of the big
cycles,[3] even though the cycles represented a small percentage of mystery play productions. Of the rest of medieval
drama, we have only five or six morality plays (three collected in one manuscript by the monks at Bury), a very few
miracle plays, and half a dozen assorted fragments.

MEDIEVAL PERFORMANCES

To what extent do these preserved texts reflect the kinds of
drama actually performed in medieval England? And to
what extent do their numbers indicate the relative frequency
with which different types of plays were acted? Records of
performance suggest that there is no close correlation on either score. For instance, we have about half of all the Corpus
Christi cycles known to have been acted in England. But we
have none of the many folk plays which can be certainly
dated before 1500. And not only do the surviving manuscripts falsely suggest that Corpus Christi plays[4] were the
most common form of medieval drama, but they also suggest that the normal Corpus Christi play was a cycle play,
which was not the case either. Only about one in three
known Corpus Christi plays was a cycle, and possibly only
one in six, depending on whether York, Chester, and New-

1. shorter plays, typically in dialogue, that developed from moralities but gradually involved more secular plots   2. also known as miracle plays, they presented biblical stories or reenacted saints' lives   3. a collection of mystery plays, often performed over
the course of several days   4. Corpus Christi was a late-spring feast day that was often marked by the performance of miracle plays.

castle actually had cycle plays before 1500; the majority were single plays of uncertain or inconsistent subject matter. If we had all the pertinent records, the percentage of cycle plays would appear even smaller, for we are probably aware of all the cycle plays but of only a fraction of the single plays.

Combining the sparse information given in E.K. Chambers' *Mediaeval Stage* with the records collected for the Malone Society publications, we can arrive at a rough estimate of the percentages of different kinds of plays acted in medieval England. Before 1500, 16% of the plays with known subject or type were acted at Corpus Christi; 26% were non-cycle mysteries acted mostly at Christmas and Easter; 26% were saints' lives and other miracle plays; 31% were folk plays—almost double the Corpus Christi plays and far more in number of performances; of morality plays, there is not a single recorded performance in the middle ages. . . .

Their total absence from the records does not necessarily mean that moralities were never acted, but it does suggest that they could not have represented a very popular or significant segment of medieval drama. In our laudable desire to find medieval roots for Renaissance drama we are, I suspect, looking in the wrong direction. Perhaps we ought to be looking at the kinds of plays we now know to have been most commonly acted in the middle ages—folk plays and miracle plays. The shortage of extant texts makes the task rather difficult, but we know enough about both types of drama that it should be possible to see some very clear areas of influence on Renaissance comedy, tragedy, and history plays.

THE MEDIEVAL IMPACT ON RENAISSANCE PLAYS

Professional comedy was in existence very much longer than was previously thought, at least as early as the fourteenth century. It is not likely to have been imitative of classical comedy, which seems not to have affected English drama before the sixteenth century. And it certainly was not influenced by the comic episodes of the much later Corpus Christi cycles, any influence being more likely in the other direction. Whatever it was like, early professional comedy had to be written for two and three man troupes, or four at the most. One would expect simple situation comedy, something on the order of John Heywood's *Johan the Husband*. The fragment dated about 1300 known as *Clerico et Puella* [anon.], for two or perhaps three actors, may be an early example.

Thematically, Renaissance comedy seems to be closely related to the medieval folk plays. The relationship has been noted before, but usually in a roundabout way. Robert Potter has outlined the evidence supporting a strong influence of the mummers' plays[5] on morality drama. Potter then finds an influence of the moralities on subsequent playwrights, including Ben Jonson. But were the moralities not considered to be intermediaries, the influence of the mummers' plays on Elizabethan comedy would be much easier to see. The general pattern of a threat of disaster followed by redemption and rebirth is observable in most Renaissance comedies. In some, there is the magical "cure" effected by a counterpart of the doctor (the ghost of Jack in George Peele's *The Old Wives' Tale,* for instance, or Oberon with his love-juice in William Shakespeare's *Midsummer Night's Dream*). In others, there is even an apparently miraculous resurrection from death (Sebastian in *Twelfth Night,* Claudio in *Measure for Measure,* Imogen and Posthumus in *Cymbeline,* Hermione in *Winter's Tale* [all by Shakespeare]). It is not my business to develop such influences here, but only to suggest that they exist.

Perhaps the clearest medieval influence on Renaissance drama is that of the saints' lives on history plays. The miracles were the most numerous, popular, and widely varied of medieval religious dramas. They also had the longest tradition among the fully developed plays: the earliest performance of Christian drama on record in England is of a St. Catherine play before 1119 at Dunstable, and the last saints' lives were still being performed at the beginning of Elizabeth's reign. Almost none of the many British saints' lives plays are extant, but we know by numerous continental examples that they were structurally very like the Elizabethan history plays. The only surviving play about a British saint, the Cornish *Life of St. Meriasek* [anon.] of about 1475, will demonstrate the structural similarity. This play dramatizes four periods in the life of Meriasek, including his connection with Cambourne, where the play was acted. Alternating with these four episodes are dramatizations of stories from Jacob de Voragine's *Legenda Aurea*[6] about St. Silvester and the Emperor Constantine, and the interlude of St. Mary and

---

5. plays, often in pantomime, which were performed by masked actors   6. translated as "Golden Legend," a collection of legendary lives of the saints

the Woman's Son. Thus we find a main plot alternating with a sub-plot which parallels and mirrors the main plot but is not closely related to it except by one anachronistic connection—much in the manner of *Edward III* [anon.[7]] or Shakespeare's *Henry IV* or almost any other Elizabethan history play. Like the authors who followed him, this playwright remains true to the spirit of history while feeling free to rearrange events, reassign action to different personages, telescope history and introduce anachronisms. He develops a variety of character types, from humble priest to raging tyrant. And he provides exciting action: two pitched battles and two fights with dragons, among other events, along with the threatened mass murder of 3140 innocent children to provide Constantine's famous bloodbath. There is not as much action, perhaps, as in Christopher Marlowe's *Massacre at Paris,* but it is considerably more exciting than *Mundus et Enfans* [anon.].

Even the Elizabethan history plays which seem most likely to be descended from the moralities would, I should think, have derived a good deal more that was useful in terms of character, structure, and thematic development from such miracle plays. Clearly, a play so important to later historical drama as *The Famous Victories of Henry the Fifth* [anon.] owes more to the typical miracle play, with its emphasis on conversion and subsequent miracles wrought by the reformed hero, than it does to morality plays. And surely *Woodstock* [anon.], Marlowe's *Edward II,* and Shakespeare's *Richard II* have more in common with *King Robert of Sicily* than with *The Castle of Perseverance* [both anon.]. Each of these histories deals with an English monarch who, like King Robert, is brought low by his own willfulness and lack of humility. One might add that the story of Robert of Sicily almost inevitably brings to mind Shakespeare's version of *King Lear,* where for the same reasons Lear is reduced to rags and the company of fools and madmen if not to being made into a fool himself. *King Lear,* of course, has many additional parallels with the mummers' plays, both in structure and in specific details of action, from an old man's legacies to his ungrateful children to the mock trial and the trial by combat and to the miraculous cure and "resurrection" of Lear and Gloucester.

7. anonymous, although parts have been credited to Christopher Marlowe and Shakespeare

But the two kinds of influence, saints' lives and mummers' plays, would seem ultimately to be a single source of inspiration. For the saints' lives may have been as popular as they were at least partly because they gave a specifically Christian sanction to the action of the mummers' plays. That is, the stories of miracles performed by saints following their martyrdoms provide firm evidence of a resurrection more significant (because eternal) than the standard physical resurrection . . . in the mummers' plays. Miracle plays perform the same ritual purpose, in short, but they also incorporate the Christian beliefs which turn the seasonal miracle into an everlasting one.

When one considers that the saints' lives continued until well into the sixteenth century and that the folk plays never did completely die out, one can see a continuous line of development from medieval to high Renaissance drama, even though most of the extant early Tudor plays are court or school plays. A drama such as Henry Medwall's *Fulgens et Lucres,* while probably written for private performance and requiring more actors than a professional troupe could muster, seems to borrow ideas both from the professional drama with its alternating serious and comic episodes (compare even a late play such as Thomas Middleton and William Rowley's *The Changeling*), and the folk drama with its mummers' dance, challenges, . . . mock combat, and apparent death and resurrection. What is harder to find is any clear medieval model for Renaissance tragedy. Nowhere in the records is there any reference to performance of a tragedy in the middle ages either by professionals or by amateurs. In fact, I am not aware of any specific evidence that tragedy was performed in Britain earlier than 1554, at Magdalen College, Oxford. Are we therefore forced to conclude that [Roman dramatist] Seneca was the chief influence on Renaissance tragedy? Or that the only medieval influences were the moralities, despite their virtual nonexistence and, with their aim of promulgating the sacrament of penance, singularly inappropriate as models for tragedy of character employing the method of exempla rather than allegory?

THE THOMAS À BECKET PLAYS

I should like to suggest that we are not reduced to either expedient, and that there is abundant evidence, if I interpret it correctly, that tragedy was being acted in England from the twelfth right into the sixteenth century. Unfortunately, the texts which would prove the contention have all been destroyed, and the argument will have to be from antecedent probability. I am referring to the Thomas à Becket plays.[8]

Although the records of medieval drama are disappointingly meager except in the case of the big Corpus Christi and Whitsun cycles and although the records of only a few counties have thus far been systematically collected, it is becoming clear that more plays on Thomas à Becket were performed than on any other subject except the traditional Christmas and Easter plays. There was a play on St. Thomas in London as early as 1182, shortly after his death. The earliest recorded drama in East Anglia was a Thomas à Becket play at Bishop's Lynn in 1385. The earliest play with a known title in Kent was on St. Thomas, at Ham in 1453; Canterbury, as one might expect, presented St. Thomas plays yearly over a long period. And there were others, as at Norwich, Bungay, and Mildenhall, at least as late as 1539.

After Henry VIII personally and firmly demoted Becket from the ranks of saints, these plays understandably disappeared—along with virtually every other English miracle drama. But even without an extant text, it is possible to surmise with considerable confidence what the St. Thomas plays were like; that is, we can presuppose as accurately as we could about plays on Abraham and Isaac had we no extant mysteries on that subject. For it happens that, while we have numerous versions of the life of St. Thomas, from the *South English Legendary* to an Icelandic version, they are all remarkably similar even when not dependent upon one another; and these lives would necessarily have been the sources for the plays.

The lives of St. Thomas differ from other medieval saints' lives in two important respects: they are specific and historical rather than fabulous and general, and they are not chiefly concerned either with a wondrous conversion or with miracles performed after that conversion or related to the saint's death. What these lives do present is the story of a man who was good, brilliant, and promising from early childhood and who rose to be second in temporal power and chief in spiritual power in the kingdom. From this position of eminence, he was forced to choose between church and

8. Becket, the archbishop of Canterbury, was murdered in 1170.

state during the power struggle of Henry II's reign, and his choice resulted in his being murdered by supporters of the king. The materials presented in the sources are thus ready-made for tragedy: the protagonist falls, not because he is mortal like Everyman[9] or because he is overwhelmed by external forces but because, after considerable soul-searching, he makes a crucial moral choice and abides by it. Like Antigone,[10] his choice may be the right one (at least in the view of his biographers), but it still will cost him his life and he knows that it will do so. And also like Antigone, Becket wins his victory by sacrificing his life. The story is a tragedy in the finest and most uplifting tradition. It is difficult to imagine how a dramatist, working from such material, could have distorted it into any form other than tragedy. It is even harder to imagine that every playwright in the middle ages who worked with this story was equally determined to turn it from what it was into something different. One is almost forced to the conclusion that at least some of the Thomas à Becket plays were genuine tragedies. . . .

THE DEVELOPMENT OF ENGLISH TRAGEDY

One cannot, of course, go beyond the hypothesis until—and if—an authentic Thomas à Becket play is discovered. But if these plays were, as seems to me likely, true tragedies, we have a tradition of English tragedy extending over a period of 360 years and to within fifteen years of the first recorded tragedy in 1554. It is possible, then, that English tragedy was a continuously developing form from the twelfth century all the way through the Renaissance. At any rate, it no longer seems safe to echo earlier critics who contended that there was no medieval dramatic tragedy.

As it is more convenient to argue for dramatic influences if one has the texts before him, the few moralities we have seem more fruitful than the many miracles we do not have. And if both moralities and later drama happened to be influenced by now-extinct folk plays, the appearance will be that it was the extant moralities which influenced the later plays. We are not likely at this date to uncover dramatic manuscripts which will prove otherwise: the mummers' plays may never have been written down at all, and the

9. the main character of the most well-known morality play   10. the title character in a play by Greek dramatist Sophocles

Becket plays probably all suffered the fate of other "idola-trous" literature at the Reformation—Becket being more likely than any other saint to have plays about him de-stroyed. For he was not merely a latter-day saint but one who achieved martyrdom by refusing to recognize the tem-poral powers of an English monarch in spiritual matters. But we should keep in mind that both folk and miracle plays had a very long and widespread popular tradition, existing long before any morality plays were written and outlasting them as well. There is certainly no need to see moralities as links between medieval and Renaissance drama on chrono-logical grounds—nor, so far as I can see, any need to do so on thematic or structural grounds.

Common Plots in Elizabethan Drama

Madeleine Doran

Madeleine Doran argues that plot-making in Elizabethan drama borrows from Roman, medieval, and Italian plays. Four common themes in Elizabethan plots with these antecedents are good opposing evil, the fall of the hero and the rise of the villain, revenge and counter revenge, and comic intrigue. Elizabethan plays which utilize such themes include William Shakespeare's *Much Ado About Nothing, Julius Caesar*, and *The Taming of the Shrew*. While the Elizabethan dramas use these standard plots, they are also more sophisticated and utilize characters that are more fully developed. Doran was a professor emerita of English at the University of Wisconsin at Madison, a poet, a dramatist, and the author of works such as *Endeavors of Art: A Study of Form in Elizabethan Drama*, from which this article is excerpted.

For help in plot-making the English relied on traditional types of story and motive. Underneath the sophistication and the complexity of mature Elizabethan drama we may still see a few familiar patterns of conflict that began early and lasted long. I shall discuss four of the commonest themes and techniques of dramatic opposition—the opposition of good and evil, the cyclic rise and fall pattern of *De casibus* tragedy, the motivation of action and counter-action by revenge, and the intrigue technique of Roman comedy.

GOOD AND EVIL

Opposition between good and evil was a theme both of romance and of moral play. Medieval romance was not very helpful . . . in teaching coherence of dramatic action. It had one aspect, however, which deserves remarking in this con-

Excerpted from *Endeavors of Art*, by Madeleine Doran. Copyright ©1954 by the Regents of the University of Wisconsin. Reprinted by permission of The University of Wisconsin Press.

nection. Conflict was typically between a noble hero and a malignant adversary—giant, dragon, enchanter, Saracen[1]— symbolic in a rather general, conventional way of right and wrong, good and evil, beauty and ugliness, or the like. Emphasis was on the story and the contestants in their own right; the ethical implications were simple and might be taken for granted, though they were sometimes pointed up in Christian terms. Saints' legends, for all their nonsecular emphasis, were cut out of the same cloth. To this kind of thing was readily assimilable the explicit opposition of virtues and vices in the morality play. We can see the joining, unfused, in *Mary Magdalene, Common Conditions, Appius and Virginia* [all anon.], and other early plays in which conduct in stories of romantic origin and flavor is motivated by abstract figures from the moralities.

Satan, usually through a subordinate devil or a representative vice, was of course the principal adversary in the moralities. But he was hardly a new figure on the stage. In the grand scheme of the mystery cycles—the fall of man and his redemption—the conflict between good and evil had always been implicit, though doubtless not much attended to by the ordinary viewers of the plays; sometimes, in plays on particular subjects like the Fall, the Temptation of Christ, or the Harrowing of Hell, in which Satan must appear as a visible antagonist, the conflict had become actual and immediate.

The conception of the evil adversary never altogether died out of English renaissance drama, either comedy or tragedy. Romantic comedy and tragi-comedy continued to have their malicious villains. If Sacrapant and Friar Bungay[2] seem too old-fashioned and anachronistic to be good examples, consider Don John of William Shakespeare's *Much Ado About Nothing,* Antonio of Shakespeare's *The Tempest,* Megra of John Fletcher's *Philaster,* the Queen and Iachimo of Shakespeare's *Cymbeline.* Don John is a specially illuminating example, because he appears to have no adequate reason to destroy Hero and is hence unsatisfactory to modern taste. But he need not be particularly motivated, for he belongs to an ancient and familiar convention, that of the malicious worker of evil who throws obstacles in the path of true love and virtue.

1. a medieval European term for an Arab or Muslim   2. characters from George Peele's *The Old Wive's Tale* and Robert Greene's *Friar Bacon and Friar Bungay,* respectively

Nor did Satan ever wholly desert English tragedy. Although the old external conflict of the moralities between
the virtues and the vices—the former instigated by reason as
the instrument of God, and the latter prompted by the un-
controlled passions as the instrument of Satan—became in
part internal and psychological and no longer so simple in
its issues, the sense of an evil adversary to man's good persisted. The adversary appears in Christopher Marlowe's [*The
Tragical History of Doctor*] *Faustus* in a literal way, and the
conflict within Faustus is exhibited in the old morality form
of external debate between the contenders for his soul. The
adversary appears in Shakespeare's *Othello* more masked in
symbolism, but none the less recognizable:

> I look down at his feet. But that's a fable.

And the conflict is expressed in terms of the passions warring within Othello's breast. . . .

In Shakespeare there is a much stronger sense of responsibility in character than in some of his contemporaries, especially George Chapman and John Webster, in whom there
is, hardly more pity, but certainly more apology, for irrational passion. Even in Shakespeare, however, the foe is
without as well as within. Othello's goodness is sufficient to
meet and conquer any recognizable evil; the terrible thing is
that the evil he meets is not recognizable for what it is.

Medieval romance and pageant, then, furnished the conception of dramatic conflict between a hero and a malignant
adversary; the morality play, the same thing expressed in
theological and ethical terms and with the conflict external
in representation but in implication internal as well. The religious drama generally, both mystery and miracle play, had
for centuries given representational vividness to the conflict
between man in his fallen state and his sleepless enemy.

DE CASIBUS TRAGEDY

The medieval conception of tragedy as the fall of a man of
wealth or power at the hands of adverse fortune was inade-
quate in itself for drama unless the evil fortune was made to
appear in the form of external enemies. But the germ of
complication lay in the cyclic pattern of *De casibus* tragedy,
with one man rising as another fell. All that was necessary
for drama was to make the rise consequent upon the fall,
that is, to present the fall of the hero as engineered by a

climbing rival. The motive of ambition countered by ambition, and perhaps by revenge as well, produced a perfectly characteristic and recognizable pattern: a curve of rise and fall for the protagonist, with the fall of the protagonist crossed by the rise of the antagonist. This is the pattern of Marlowe's *Edward II*, Shakespeare's *Julius Caesar*, and Ben Jonson's *Sejanus*. It was one of Shakespeare's favorite patterns; he used it, with modifications, in many of his histories, in all his Roman plays, and in *Macbeth*.

One of the ways to increase the dramatic intensity of this theme was to motivate opposition in the clash of personalities as well as in circumstances—to pit the insolent assurance of Mortimer, for instance, against the scolding vacillation of Edward; the shrewd self-control of Bolingbroke against the self-pitying irresponsibility of Richard; the cold, rather mean, competence of Octavius Caesar against the warm extravagant rashness of Antony.[3] Such clash of character complicated the old simple pattern of Fortune's turning wheel. It did not necessarily rob her of her power, only gave her a plausible means to work in a world of men's wills, mutually irritant, jealous, or emulous, and perpetually at variance.

REVENGE PLAYS

The motive of revenge, sometimes present in *De casibus* tragedy, has to be considered in its own right, since it was to prove one of the most fruitful of all motives for dramatic opposition. Senecan[4] tragedy appears to have given it its impetus on the English stage, but it was a rather ubiquitous motive to be found as well in Mirror stories, in Greek drama and myth, in modern Italian *novelle* and plays, all familiar as source material. Doubtless with Seneca's *Thyestes* and *Thebais* in mind, Thomas Sackville and Thomas Norton used revenge as a major complicating motive of their politically directed, pseudo-historical plot in *Gorboduc* (1562). Thomas Hughes imposed a more obviously Senecan variety of revenge on the Arthurian legend in his *Misfortunes of Arthur* (ca. 1587). Into *Gismond of Salerne* (ca. 1567–68) revenge came with the source story from Giovanni Boccaccio. In all these plays the movement is rather simple: one action provoking a counter-action of revenge, that in turn leading to

---

3. characters from *Edward II*, Shakespeare's *Richard II*, and Shakespeare's *Julius Caesar*, respectively   4. referring to Roman dramatist Seneca

THE POPULARITY OF THE REVENGE PLOT

*Revenge plots are a common motif in Elizabethan drama.
Literary critic T.B. Tomlinson notes their popularity and
considers the fate of the revenge protagonist. According to
Tomlinson, the protagonist's schemes against the society and
people who have wronged him frequently lead to his downfall.*

Revenge dominates Elizabethan play-writing as no motif has
ever dominated a period of English literature after the mediaeval Romance. Metaphysical verse, Augustan moral epistles,
nineteenth-century family romances—for better or for worse
none of these has the unity and coherence given to a large
group of Elizabethan and Jacobean plays by the Revenge plot.
Even when, as in John Webster and Cyril Tourneur, Revenge
impinges on wider issues, it still manages to retain an almost
separable identity. The nearest parallel to this situation would
probably be with Restoration Heroic Tragedy, where the sense
of structure, over a generation or so of writers, was almost as
complete and as mandatory; but here the resulting product
is irrevocably minor. The modern detective story, from the
'twenties onwards, is another comparison often cited, but it
is one which, by virtue of its even more obvious limitations,
only succeeds in demonstrating more clearly still the uniqueness of the position held by the apparently melodramatic
Revenge plot.

Thus the period from Thomas Kyd and Christopher Marlowe to John Ford produces a number of plays which stress—
though admittedly in widely differing ways—the call to revenge an injustice inflicted by society, one's fellow human
beings, the universe itself, or even, as in Shakespeare's *Hamlet*, by something still less tangible and definable. Typically,
the protagonist (villain or hero or both) is urged to action as
much by a general *malaise* as by the specific wrongs he or his
mistress has suffered; he is, like the contemporary Malcontent, isolated from and by a corrupt society, though in his isolation he nevertheless represents the human condition; and
he is generally driven to act, not as [Shakespeare's King] Lear
'acts', in open rage, but rather with . . . cunning irony. . . . The
'irony' of Revenge is indeed one of its most characteristic
traits: in Revenge plots the hero must rely on his own wit to
enforce his 'justice', and often he is in the end caught by the
very cunning of his own plots.

T.B. Tomlinson, *A Study of Elizabethan and Jacobean Tragedy.* Cambridge, England: Cambridge University Press, 1964.

catastrophe either directly or through a further act of counter-revenge. There is little, if any, manipulation by intrigue. But the Gismond story, with its motives of love, honor, and jealousy, and its action of secrecy, surprise, and deadliness, is of a type that invited exploitation of the revenge motive. This sort of situation and motivation would develop towards more and more intricate knots of revenge and counter-revenge, plotted by intrigue—in short, towards Thomas Kyd's *The Spanish Tragedy*, Shakespeare's *Titus Andronicus*, and *The Revenger's Tragedy* [author unknown].

Greater tragic meaning came with the shift of emphasis from the mere problem of getting the revenge done to the impact of revenge on the character of the revenger. The handling of the ghost as motivator throws this shift into relief. In the simplest pattern, following *Thyestes*, the necessity of the revenge action somehow resides in the ghost; revenge is first of all his concern, and it is enough for him to appear for the action to begin. In Seneca's play, the spirit of Thyestes is tormented by Megaera so to inspire his nephews with rage, fury, and discord that they will continue the chain of crimes begun by him. In Robert Wilmot's *The Misfortunes of Arthur*, the ghost of Gorlois, wanting vengeance on the family of Uther Pendragon for the seduction of his wife, prophesies the events which lead eventually to the mutual self-destruction of Arthur and Mordred. In *Locrine* (ca. 1591) [usually attributed to Robert Greene] the ghost of Albanact drives Humber, his slayer, to commit suicide. Although *The Spanish Tragedy* keeps the outward frame of this pattern, in that the ghost of Andreas calls for revenge and sits on the stage to watch the destruction of his enemies, the real motivation has changed. There is something of the conventional assumption of inevitability, it is true, in the way in which Bel-Imperia, on hearing of the death of her sweetheart, begins automatically to set about to revenge him. But with Hieronimo's problem of avenging his murdered son, we are wholly in the realm of human trouble and human character. Perhaps written under the influence of Shakespeare's *Hamlet*, the later additions to the play intensify the element of conflict in Hieronimo between unnerving and distracting grief and desire for revenge. Even in the first form of the play, however, revenge is a problem in character as well as in action; it is the germ of the thing that leads to Hamlet. In *Hamlet* the ghost is once more a genuine inciting force, but what he incites is not just the act of revenge; it is a devastating conflict in Hamlet's soul. Later ghosts—Bussy's in Chapman's *The Revenge of Bussy,* Brachiano's in Webster's *The White Devil,* Alonzo's in Thomas Middleton and William Rowley's *The Changeling*— can at best be taken only as symbolic reminders of duty to the revenger, or of guilt to the murderer. With their need as motivators gone, they have degenerated into mere mechanical survivals of an old tradition. They are the pallid ghosts of ghosts. Montferrer's ghost, in Cyril Tourneur's *The Atheist's Tragedy,* has the distinction of charging his son Charlemont *not* to avenge his death, but to follow the Christian ethic of forgiveness.

Why the motive of revenge should enjoy such popularity from the early days of Elizabethan down to Caroline times naturally provokes speculation. That it had deeply sympathetic affinities with the conditions of actual life we must suppose. Yet its very endurance, even after it had lost its vitality, as the commonest counter-motive in tragedy, suggests something besides imitative realism. Its persistence may have been to some extent owing to its great usefulness for play construction in furnishing so practicable a method of counter-action.

COMIC INTRIGUE

The counterpart of the intrigue plot in tragedy motivated by revenge is the intrigue plot of Roman and Italian comedy, in which the complicating motive is the outwitting of somebody. Again, as with the revenge motive, though the conditions of London life produced plenty of types of rogues to do the outwitting and of fools to be outwitted, one may suspect that this pattern of opposition had a dramatic usefulness irrelevant to its realism. It was a workable frame, easy to use over and over—as the monotonously repetitive situations of Italian comedy prove.

The best English comedies of this sort are freshened with many [characters] . . . who make their fantastic rogueries or stupidities seem of the stuff of human sharp practice or silliness. But characters as individual as these are, in a sense, an agreeable bonus; for the most conventional motivations in stock types, as Latin comedy illustrates, will serve to pull the strings of the intrigue. And, since the fun is in the cleverness of the manipulation, a few threads of nicely calculated coincidence to make the knot more intricate will help the plot rather than hinder it. Shakespeare's *Comedy of Errors, Taming of the Shrew* (the Bianca story), and *Merry Wives [of Windsor]*; Henry Porter's *Two Angry Women of Abingdon*; and some of Middleton's and Chapman's comedies are the happiest examples of this sort of witty plotting. . . .

Intrigue was useful, too, in the manipulation of plots of romantic adventure. For the hazards and lucky chances of fortune—the separations of twins and sweethearts, the shipwrecks, the captures by pirates, the recognitions by rings and by chests of baby garments—which are the stuff of romantic story, need something to pull them out of the straight line of successive episodes into a knot of complication. A wicked magician (or even a Prospero [from Shakespeare's *The Tempest*]) to rile up the sea at an opportune moment will work wonders for a plot.

In a purely romantic story, character in any individualized sense is no more a necessity than in a story of roguery largely worked by intrigue. For a romantic plot can coast on the conventional expectations of story for story's sake. The element of the fortuitous is generally much larger than in a plot of more "domestic" intrigue; and the characters themselves must meet standard expectations of motive: love at first sight, the pangs of jealousy or separation, natural malice or benevolence, and so on. When character is deepened, therefore, in a romantic story, it ought not to be allowed to alter the motivation seriously. Caught in the fantastic and exaggerated situations of the plot, the characters should behave convincingly; yet they must still be largely moved by the accidents of their fairy-tale world. Viola [in Shakespeare's *Twelfth Night*], in disguise as a boy and as an unwilling wooer of her own beloved's mistress, behaves with all the embarrassment, pertness, ruefulness, and wit a real Viola would in such an unlikely situation; but Viola can be extricated from her predicament only by several even more unlikely chances—the arrival on the spot of her twin brother, supposed drowned, the mistaking of him for her by the woman who loves her, and his willingness to walk into matrimony with a strange woman in the very instant of meeting her. What happens in Shakespearean romantic comedy is that fully-conceived characters give an illusion of reality to the most fantastic situations; we are presented, therefore, with a delightful and rather zany world that we yet believe in.

The Tragic Hero in Elizabethan Drama

D.J. Palmer

D.J. Palmer asserts that one of the defining characteristics of Elizabethan drama is the creation of the
tragic hero. Thomas Kyd and Christopher Marlowe
are the two playwrights chiefly responsible for the
development of this character type, although William
Shakespeare shows greater skill in his use of the
tragic hero. Hieronimo, the tragic hero of Kyd's *The
Spanish Tragedy*, seeks justice and questions the
wisdom of God. His traits are seen in Shakespearean
tragic heroes, notably Hamlet and King Lear. Marlowe's tragic heroes, such as Tamburlaine, differ
from Kyd's because they are more intellectual and
motivated by their inherent nature, not by the circumstances in which they find themselves. Richard
III is a Shakespearean character with traits reminis-
cent of Marlovian heroes. Palmer has edited a variety of books about Shakespeare.

The blood which flows so copiously from the heroes of Elizabethan tragedy is as mixed as their complex descent from
medieval and classical ancestry, yet they exemplify in their
careers a consistent, universal pattern of divine and human
justice. Tragedy was understood by the Elizabethans to
teach, and its characteristic lesson was an affirmation of
God's goodness and power in punishing the wicked and
avenging the righteous. However heterogeneous was the literary grist which came to their mill, they leavened it with
their own preconceptions and used it to enforce their tragic
moralising. Yet this admonitory intent, more grossly palpable in the plays of the early part of the period, did not necessarily produce a simplified attitude to good and evil: much
recent commentary upon Elizabethan tragedy, including the

Excerpted from "Elizabethan Tragic Heroes," by D.J. Palmer, in *Elizabethan Theatre*,
vol. 9 of Stratford-upon-Avon Studies, edited by John Russell Brown and Bernard Harris (New York: St. Martin's Press, 1967). Reprinted by permission of the original publisher, Edward Arnold, London; ©1966.

debate about Christopher Marlowe's *Tamburlaine [the Great]*, is perhaps misled by the assumption that a dramatic plot can be reduced to one or other of the common places of sixteenth-century moral doctrine. All Elizabethan tragedies in fact try to illustrate several lessons at once, by incorporating within their actions a whole series of tragic catastrophes, each with its own significance. From this point of view, therefore, the most appropriate kind of tragic hero for the Elizabethan dramatist was the figure whose progress through the play would involve as many other characters as possible, so providing opportunities for emphasising a maximum number of moral lessons. The better playwrights, of course, managed to reconcile this taste for multiplicity with dramatic unity, but it did frequently produce inconsistent characterisation of the hero, and it certainly complicated the treatment of good and evil, since one man's crime was often another's just desert.

ELEMENTS OF THE TRAGIC HERO

Even in the apparently exceptional case of Marlowe, who subordinates the moral issues of his plays to a somewhat metaphysical conception of motivation and conflict, the Elizabethan tragic hero is presented in terms of a scheme which accepts a rational and just basis for life. His plays, like those of his contemporaries, draw so much of their tragic authority from that profound awareness of humanity's mediate place between the angels and the beasts, and therefore of man's capacity for both transcendent glory and degradation. Marlowe does not contradict the more conventional teaching of other dramatists, that evil and catastrophe are explicable according to orthodox Christian belief; scepticism or a sense of an indifferent heaven may be permitted to heathens, villains, or those in despair, but such attitudes are never endorsed by the tragic scheme. It is the insistence upon tragedy as the working out of a just, ethical plan which ascribes to the Elizabethan hero a much greater scope in his control over his circumstances and in his exercise of free will than either [Roman dramatist] Seneca or the medieval tragedies of Fortune afforded. The tragic conflict in Elizabethan drama is precipitated by human forces, and, particularly in the plays of Thomas Kyd, Marlowe and their successors, the situations are resolved at the level of character, often where the hero believes he is acting as the instrument of divine purpose. As a dramatic figure, he develops within a tradition in which to an increasing degree he is responsible for, and aware of, his destiny. While Geoffrey Chaucer and John Lydgate had shown how pride, ambition, and other worldly sins greased the wheel of Fortune, the more typical Elizabethan emphasis upon moral responsibility is first reflected by the *Mirror for Magistrates* (1559) [anon.]. Here the world of the mighty is made insecure not by the blind operations of an external force, but by their own unrestrained lusts or neglect of true allegiance.

To the sixteenth century, Senecan tragedy also appeared to represent this moralised pattern of crime and punishment: one of the main difficulties in estimating Seneca's influence is their tendency to read him in the light of their own beliefs. The vindictive and arbitrary interventions of his deities, for instance, were grossly misrepresented in order to reconcile his teaching with the Christian scheme of heavenly justice, and Alexander Nevile, translating the *Oedipus* in 1563, attributed the fate of his hero to a divine judgement that is more biblical than stoic:

> Marke thou rather what is ment by the whole course of the History . . . the right high and immortall God, will never leave such horrible and detestable crimes unpunished.

> ('Preface to the Reader.')

Seneca was revered first and foremost as a moralist; no other pagan writer, according to Thomas Newton in his dedication of the *Ten Tragedies* [translation of Seneca's plays] in 1581, 'more sensibly, pithily, and bytingly layeth doune the guerdon of filthy lust, cloaked dissimulation and odious treachery.' As far as the Elizabethans were concerned, Seneca showed wickedness bringing down destruction upon its own head, and he taught them to motivate this wickedness through passions like those that convulse his characters. Ambition, the lust for revenge, and sexual passion are the chief sources of Elizabethan tragic action, and the means for making character morally responsible in the dramatic scheme. From Seneca also came such rhetorical devices as the pithy *sententiae* [aphorisms] and the speeches of lamentation and suffering which serve to heighten the sense of tragic loss and outrage. Seneca's concern with the ruler and his exercise of power naturally coincided with the Elizabethan interest in courts and princes, and with the traditional idea that the subject of tragedy ought to be a figure of high estate. Admired for his doctrine, therefore, Seneca also exerted his influence upon dramatic method.

The influence of Seneca was fertile where the ground was ready to receive him, but although seven of the ten plays then thought to be his were translated between 1559 and 1566, he was only one of the complex and disparate elements which converged in the development of the Elizabethan tragic hero. Medieval romance, the conventions of courtly pageants and the morality interludes,[1] the Bible and [Roman poet] Virgil, were also absorbed with that astonishing aptitude of the Elizabethans for harmonising the most alien and miscellaneous literary and philosophical models. The principal 'types' of tragic character were already established by the 1570's; the cunning villain, the cruel tyrant, the bereaved lover or parent, the conquering hero and the avenger, combined with each other in all possible ways, had made their appearances on the popular stage or in the academic drama. Yet the tragedies of the 1560's seem very remote as predecessors of Kyd and Marlowe, partly no doubt because so few plays have survived from the intervening years. The fact remains that the two later dramatists were received by their contemporaries as great originals, inaugurating a new phase of Elizabethan tragedy. They transformed the drama, to put it as briefly as possible, by their invention of the ironic method, and by their introduction of a plot-structure in which the final catastrophe is derived from the inner logic of character and situation, and comes as the dénouement to set the action in perspective. The plays of Kyd and Marlowe express their judgements through irony, and their protagonists are distinguished from the earlier heroes by that greater measure of awareness which endows them with spiritual grandeur. The later dramatists greatly reduce the amount of undramatic exposition and overt moralising which were features of primitive Elizabethan tragedy; triumph and catastrophe are conceived in the particularised images of the action, needing no reference to a larger world beyond the dramatised situation. Hieronimo [from Kyd's *The Spanish Tragedy*] and the Marlovian heroes are at the centre of a situation which is not fixed and static, defining them immediately as in the earlier

---

1. Interludes are plays in dialogue that usually provided ethical teachings and gradually began using more secular plots.

tragedies, but which bears them forwards towards the resolution that is needed to complete the judgement upon them. In short, Kyd and Marlowe present a new conception of the hero, not as a psychological or moral type, but as the dramatic embodiment of the tragic vision. . . .

KYD'S USE OF TRAGIC HEROES

Hieronimo plays only a secondary part in the first Act of *The Spanish Tragedy*, and indeed his situation resembles that of a minor character in Seneca, extended to heroic proportions. The figure of the bereaved father is paralleled in other tragedies by those witnesses of calamity who appear briefly but lament at length the victims of human wickedness or divine wrath. But Hieronimo's grief is not used to heighten Lorenzo's villainy or Horatio's untimely death, and as he emerges in the course of the action as the tragic hero himself, it becomes apparent Hieronimo's antecedents are more biblical than Senecan in character. He is the just and upright servant of God, suddenly overtaken by a catastrophe which leaves him so utterly destitute of redress that he almost despairs of God's justice. The play is about Hieronimo's quest for justice, and his tragic sufferings recall those of Job. Biblical echoes reverberate through the tragedy: Hieronimo's impassioned appeals to heaven are not merely rhetorical gestures of affliction and outrage; they are prayers, and they derive more from the lamentations of the psalmist than from the Senecan set speech. . . .

Biblical ideas and imagery, particularly from the Old Testament, are encountered throughout Elizabethan tragedy frequently enough, since the Bible is the record of God's judgements and of the way providence works through human affairs. Usually, however, biblical authority provides the simple scheme of absolutes according to which wickedness is overthrown and justice reasserted. But *The Spanish Tragedy* takes from the Bible itself a situation in which divine justice seems to neglect its office: like that of Job, Hieronimo's very trust in the ways of heaven is made the grounds for his agony, since he presumes too far in his faith that heaven will act according to his prayers. The wisdom and justice of God cannot be measured by human wisdom and law. The play does not directly deal with God's punishment of murder: its subject is Hieronimo, and we see him first claiming the help of God, then giving way to despair in his impatience, and determining to take matters into his own hands, though finally he accomplishes his vengeance in the belief that he is an agent of God's judgement. He ends not as a villain, therefore, turning away from God, but as the righteous man, trusting that he is accomplishing the will of heaven. . . .

Kyd's most discerning pupil was William Shakespeare, and the spirit of Hieronimo survives not only in the revenge heroes, but as a creative influence on the development of all those tragic figures who believe themselves more sinned against than sinning. The very derivative characterisation of Titus Andronicus reveals Shakespeare attempting to surpass Kyd in presenting a hero driven to the utmost extremes of suffering by his sheer helplessness, acting out the intolerable frustration of his agony in pantomime. His elaboration of Kyd's methods produces a grotesque effect which robs Titus of tragic dignity, as though Shakespeare was too engrossed by the theatrical and rhetorical problems of articulating a response to such overwhelming injustice. Richard II is a more coherent and sympathetic representative of this kind of hero. He has that capacity for a depth of suffering which extends the tragic vision of the play, and that eloquence and self-awareness, which, like Hieronimo's, serve to heighten his powerlessness and dependence on the support of heaven. Hamlet of course is a far more complex creation than Hieronimo: there is a paralysis of will as well as a suspension of situation, but his lineal connection with Kyd's hero is obvious. Like Hieronimo, he is isolated from the court at which he lives, and he inherits something of the instability, the vacillation between resolve and despair, and the alternation of trust and doubt, through which is dramatised a sense of the devious and mysterious providence governing both tragedies. Shakespeare's ultimate development of Kyd's prototype, however, is seen in King Lear, whose tragic progress raises to prodigiously greater intensity that terrible question asked of heaven by Hieronimo:

> How should we term your dealings to be just
> If you unjustly deal with those that in your justice trust?
>
> (III. ii. 10)

Lear's identification of the whole world with his torment, his confrontation with Mad Tom, 'the thing itself' on the heath, his mock trial of his pelican daughters, his meeting with the blind Gloucester on the way to Dover, and his waking vision of Cordelia as 'a soul in bliss', are anticipated as devices of characterisation by the transfiguring vision of Hieronimo, who saw in the old man who came to him for justice a projection of his own case:

> Ay, now I know thee, now thou nam'st thy son,
> Thou art the lively image of my grief:
> Within thy face, my sorrows I may see.
>
> (III. xiii. 161)

The pantomime of madness, in this scene as in *King Lear,* becomes a means of dramatising tragic recognition: it was Kyd who first turned the conventions of lamentation and distracted passion into a tragedy of spiritual revelation, embodied in the suffering of his protagonist.

MARLOVIAN TRAGIC HEROES

Tamburlaine and Faustus [from Marlowe's *The Tragical History of Doctor Faustus*] inhabit a vaster, more spacious world than Elizabethan drama had previously known, for not only do they have it more to themselves, but their passions convulse the whole universe, soaring beyond that limited sphere of action which circumscribes the lives of tyrants, revengers, and lovers. Marlowe's drama is more intellectual and metaphysical than moral in its conception of human will and action: he brings to the stage a diversity of speculative interests, notably in theology, political theory and astronomy. But his learning is not bookish adornment or scholarly affectation: it is vital to his presentation of character and tragic conflict. No other Elizabethan dramatist is both as philosophical and as exciting; what earlier hero, for instance, could have justified his ambition with the ideas which Marlowe has given to Tamburlaine?

> Nature, that fram'd us of four elements
> Warring within our breasts for regiment,
> Doth teach us all to have aspiring minds:
> Our souls, whose faculties can comprehend
> The wondrous architecture of the world,
> And measure every wandering planet's course,
> Still climbing after knowledge infinite,
> And always moving as the restless spheres,
> Wills us to wear ourselves and never rest,
> Until we reach the ripest fruit of all,
> That perfect bliss and sole felicity,
> The sweet fruition of an earthly crown.
>
> (I, *Tam.*, II. vii. 18)

The motives which drive Tamburlaine and Faustus do not arise from a particular situation, from an interaction between character and circumstance: their passions are self-generated. It is the essential nature of these heroes which Marlowe dramatises; there needs no Vice or any external mechanism to propel them along the course they choose. They are not creatures of deed or occasion, they themselves create the situations in which they exist. This intellectual temper of Marlowe's tragedy, his singleness of vision in liberating character from every thing but will-power, produce that sense of power and magnificence which his heroes convey. As Tamburlaine's speech explains, they are conceived dynamically, moving in an action which encompasses the whole creation. . . .

Nevertheless death in Marlovian tragedy is the final victor, whether it comes with sudden terror and violence, or whether, as in *Tamburlaine,* the hero is at last vanquished by Nature alone. The sense of mortality is felt with peculiar intensity, as the power which ultimately extinguishes all heroic pride and aspiration, the inevitable end which irreconcilably contradicts man's unlimited will and infinite desires: 'What art thou, Faustus, but a man condemn'd to die?' Quite alien to Marlowe's conception of the tragic hero is the Shakespearian implication of values which transcend mortality, where the death of the protagonist becomes his victory rather than his defeat.

The development of the ironic method by Kyd and Marlowe enabled them to define and resolve the tragic issues through the inner logic of character and situation. Although Marlowe's rather metaphysical conception of dramatic conflict left little room for a sense of mystery or religious awe in his plays, he was a much greater poet than Kyd, and the sheer impact of his rhetoric made him the dominant influence of the early 1590's. To *Tamburlaine* probably belongs the dubious honour of being the most imitated of all Elizabethan plays. . . .

SHAKESPEARE'S IMPROVEMENTS

Shakespeare does not seem to have been as strongly attracted by the Tamburlaine figure as by Barabbas [the title character in Marlowe's *The Jew of Malta*], and Aaron the Moor in *Titus Andronicus* is the first of a long line of Shakespearian villains, who like Barabbas play it cool, revel in their outrageous stratagems, and speak with the blunt pugnacity of the low style. Richard III adds charm and brilliance to the part, and with profounder psychological insight Shakespeare derives from Richard's deformity a strain of self-mockery which borders upon self-disgust. Though Shakespeare was not a great innovator in dramatic technique, he was highly resourceful and ready to adapt to his own purposes the prevailing fashions of his day. He was an acute critic of style, and while he used the available rhetorical models of Kyd and Marlowe, he did so with a certain detachment. Richard III, and the Bastard Faulconbridge in *King John,* are both characterised as heroes who parody the heavy tragic style of other characters, and consequently they possess an extra dimension of awareness. Similarly, Romeo is first presented as the conventional romantic lover before he meets Juliet, and thereafter the contrast helps to individualise him. Romeo in fact is transformed from a hero of comedy into a tragic hero, and Shakespeare's fondness for using and simultaneously abusing conventional style is a feature of his comedies as well, from *Love's Labour's Lost* to *As You Like It.* The satire directed towards Pistol and Hotspur in *Henry IV* suggests that by about 1598 the Marlovian rhetoric had had its day, for Shakespeare at least. What Shakespeare learned from Plutarch in composing *Julius Caesar* is reflected in the greater subtlety and detail with which character and motive are there presented. Shakespeare was following a master of psychological analysis, and the result was a development in the complexity of his art which left his earlier models far behind in its depth and realism.

Multiples Scenes, Characters, and Plots in Elizabethan Drama

Jonas A. Barish

Jonas A. Barish argues that a key characteristic of
Elizabethan drama is its comprehensiveness. This
comprehensiveness, or multiplicity, includes aspects
such as a stage that can represent a variety of locales, a large cast of characters from many social
classes, and double plots. This multiplicity makes
Elizabethan drama a unique style that is much different from its ancient predecessors or from the theater that followed it. Prior to his death in 1998, Barish was an authority on Ben Jonson and William
Shakespeare and a historian of the theater. His book
The Antitheatrical Prejudice details the Western
world's hostility toward the theater.

Elizabethan drama might be considered to be unique in a
number of ways, but I should like to speak only of a single
familiar way, the full uniqueness of which may perhaps be
easy to overlook. I refer to its multiplicity or comprehensiveness, and I would contrast it rapidly in that respect with
three of its main rivals in the theater of Western Europe: the
drama of the Greeks, that of neoclassical France toward the
end of the seventeenth century, and that of modern Europe
in its first or naturalistic phase as pioneered by Henrik Ibsen, Johan August Strindberg, and Anton Chekhov.

THE STAGE

We can start with the physical stage. Whether the Elizabethan theater derives from pageant wagons, or the trestle
stages of traveling fairs, or from gaming houses, or inn-
yards, or architectural structures like city gates and funerary
monuments, or from the baldachinos and pavilions in Re-

Excerpted from "The Uniqueness of Elizabethan Drama," by Jonas A. Barish, *Comparative Drama*, Summer 1977. Reprinted by permission of the editors of *Comparative Drama*.

naissance paintings, what evolves is a complex playing area, with a central platform, an alcove or discovery space at the rear, flanked by doors, a trap door leading to a cellarage below, a balcony or balustraded space above, with possibly a second level above that, and on the platform itself a pair of great columns that divide the stage. We have a versatile, multiple playing space which can represent locales such as a field, a castle, a city wall, a ship's deck, a forest, a desert, a cave, a cell, a tavern, a hall of state, or a street, in free alternation or succession. Characters can wander in from one door and out another, lean out of windows or emerge from the alcove, skulk behind pillars or peer from over arrases, and they may occupy two or more parts of the stage simultaneously. One of the most striking effects in Elizabethan drama comes from this last-named feature, as in the parley scenes in historical plays, when besieging armies stationed on the platform challenge the defenders of a town or castle situated above, or scenes of overhearing, in which characters lurking above, or behind pillars, eavesdrop on others—perhaps, as in Act V of William Shakespeare's *Troilus and Cressida,* being themselves eavesdropped on in turn—or scenes in which something is going on below stage as well as at platform level, like the cellarage sequence in Shakespeare's *Hamlet.*

If we compare all this with the fixed scene, or *skaena,* of the Greek theater, often representing a palace door, as in Sophocles' *Oedipus* or with the fixed scene of the French neoclassic stage, usually an antechamber of the palace, as in [French dramatist] Jean Racine's *Britannicus* or *Bérénice* or *Phèdre,* into which come and go only those characters who have essential business there, or with the tasteless bourgeois parlor of Ibsen, with its expressive clutter, perhaps permitting a bare glimpse of some world beyond—a fjord, a millstream, a townscape with steeple—we can see that in these other cases the fixed stage creates a sense of high focus. The action with which we are concerned is locked to the place on which our gaze is fixed, and whatever occurs elsewhere will have to be reported by messenger or some similar device of secondary narration.

On the Elizabethan stage, even when the action takes place entirely on a single island, as in Shakespeare's *The Tempest,* it still suggests fluidity and dispersal rather than concentration. It moves us hither and yon over the island, refusing to fasten itself to one spot. Probably Ben Jonson's *The Alchemist* comes closest, of Elizabethan plays, to confining itself to a fixed site, yet it does so for a special and highly eccentric purpose: to create a sense of abnormal pressure, of something bursting at the seams and threatening to explode. The rascally alchemists use the stage doors as places into which they can thrust inopportune clients, so as to make room for new arrivals who cannot be put off, so that what we see is not so much the confinement of a story to its natural locus in a single room as a multiple action deliberately *crammed* into a smaller space than it can naturally occupy, with the result that at length, like the overheated furnace and burning retorts themselves, the whole plot goes up *in fumo*, in a terrific cataclysm, after which the outside world at length comes pouring in, taking its comical revenge on the absurdity of the unity of place.

SPACE AND TIME

Spatial restriction, on the Greek and French and modern stages, entails (or imposes) severe temporal restriction. As the action unfolds before the single palace door, or in the palace peristyle, or the bourgeois parlor, it tends to limit itself sharply in time to what can be presented as a more or less continuous process, unfolding before our eyes with a minimum of gaps. This produces the brevity and intensity of what we may call Aristotelian drama. We start close to the climax. We learn about the past through devices of recapitulation and retrospection. We encounter the action only when it has become white-hot. There is no time left for digression or excursion, only for the swift completion of what is already in motion, the speeding of an arrow, long since shot from its bow, into its target—only the few hours in which the fate of Oedipus is decided, or that of Antigone or Philoctetes, or in which Britannicus or Phèdre meet their dooms, or the few days in which Nora Helmer or Mrs. Alving or Hedda Gabler come to terms with their lives and take their resolutions for the future.[1] We need hardly recall Philip Sidney's whimsical lament over the geographical licentiousness of the theater of his day and its promiscuous ways with time, or Ben Jonson's raillery about York and Lancaster's long jars,

---

1. Oedipus, Antigone, and Philoctetes were title characters in Sophocles' plays. Britannicus and Phèdre are title characters in Racine plays. Nora Helmer, Mrs. Alving, and Hedda Gabler were in the Ibsen plays *A Doll House*, *Ghosts*, and *Hedda Gabler*, respectively.

or Shakespeare's apology for the temerity of his epic enterprise in *Henry V.* What is plain, when we compare Elizabethan habits with those of other stages and other epochs, is that the shameless Elizabethan stage tries to do everything. It refuses to recognize anything as beyond its powers. It crushes decades into minutes and shrinks great empires to a few feet of square board with godlike casualness.

It must be partly this voracious appetite for space and time that gives it such a striking affinity for magic, as in Robert Greene's *Friar Bacon and Friar Bungay,* or Christopher Marlowe's [*The Tragical History of*] *Doctor Faustus,* or Thomas Dekker's *Old Fortunatus,* or Shakespeare's *Macbeth.* With the literalizing of dreams of flight, of fantasies of transformation, of clairvoyance and clairaudience, and of invisibility, with the annulment of time through the conjuring up of past and future, the whole spatial and temporal universe is brought within the compass of the playhouse. The spectators are invited to share, along with the characters, the dizzying exhilaration of traversing the cosmos in a matter of seconds, of visiting the remote past and journeying into the indiscernible future from a position of absolute security. The other theaters aim at compression and selectivity, at making a little stand for a lot. The Elizabethans wish to drag the whole lot bodily onto the stage. The other theaters hedge themselves about with exclusions and taboos. The really exciting actions, the violence, the sensationalism, the amorous encounters, the magical occurrences, all happen, as [French novelist] Victor Hugo complained, frustratingly offstage. Only the Elizabethans, with their split-level stage, their dumb shows, gods, and ghosts, their gluttony for spectacular effects, try to make everything at once visible, audible, and palpable.

LARGE CASTS

Their plays tend, in consequence, to use large casts of characters. An average Greek tragedy will contain half a dozen or so speaking parts plus a chorus. Racinian tragedy rarely exceeds seven personages—three principals, three confidants, and a slave or servant or messenger. In the modern theater, Strindberg's *The Father* contains eight characters, *Miss Julie* three. *Hedda Gabler* has six, *Uncle Vanya* nine. Shakespeare's *Henry VI, Part II,* by contrast, includes somewhere in the neighborhood of forty-five designated roles plus a bewildering array of supernumeraries: lords, ladies, attendants, petitioners, aldermen, herald, beadle, sheriff, officers, citizens, prentices, falconers, guards, soldiers, rebels, and messengers. The Elizabethan stage specializes in crowd scenes. The choruses of Greek or Senecan drama can hardly be said to constitute a crowd, such as we find at the Capulets' ball or at the court of Denmark. Still less do they compose a mob, such as we find in the street scenes of Shakespeare's *Julius Caesar* or Shakespeare's *Coriolanus*. Crowds and mobs, interestingly enough, in Elizabethan plays tend to individuate themselves, to decompose into Hob and Dick, First and Second Citizen, so that we feel them both as a horde, with an almost oppressive group identity, and also as collections of discrete individuals, each with his own passions and idiosyncrasies. When Racine needs a crowd, as in *Bérénice*, or Ibsen, as in *An Enemy of the People*, they keep them as severely off-stage as would Sophocles or Seneca.

The craving for completeness leads Elizabethan playwrights to differentiate their characters not only temperamentally but also socially, to make a practice of including representatives of every social level and mingling them freely on the stage. Final scenes in Shakespearean comedy bring the whole community, from king to commoner, together for some climactic recognition or some communal festivity, while in tragedy the society is likely to be gathered together at some point to witness or perform some painful, crucial rite, as in the forum scene of *Julius Caesar* or the play scene in Shakespeare's *Hamlet*. Jonson's comic endings involve the community in a judgment scene, in which rewards and penalties are meted out by some high tribunal before which the rest of the cast is assembled, while in Jacobean tragedy it becomes nearly formulaic for an authority figure such as a Duke or a newly crowned heir to march in and restore order at the end. The effect at such moments is always to enlarge the focus, to expand the vision, to create a sense of plenitude and inclusiveness, whereas in the other kind of play the tendency is for the focus to narrow to only those characters who are central and indispensable to the story: Prometheus [from the Aeschylus play] alone on his rock, Thésée bending over the lifeless body of Phèdre, Mrs. Alving staring helplessly into space as Osvald demands the sun, or Chekhov's three sisters clinging in desperation to one another as the regiment marches off to its new quarters.

ELIZABETHAN PLOTS AND LANGUAGE

The copious cast of an Elizabethan play, moreover, spanning the social spectrum as it does, is characteristically set to performing actions both numerous and complicated, to the point where after 1600 a play without a double plot becomes almost anomalous. Even when one cannot find a multiple plot according to strict definition, one nevertheless finds a play to be loaded with incident, swollen with episode and subsidiary scene and secondary characters. And again we can set this alongside the tight, spare construction of classical plays, with their preference for the single line, their avoidance of episodes that don't grow inevitably out of each other, or of French plays, with their even closer concatenation of events, or of Ibsenian drama, with its unrelenting pressure of passion and revelation. Most traditional drama, indeed, works by trying to maintain and step up the pressure. Elizabethan drama deliberately throws itself let-up punches, interrupts linear movement in order to go off on tangents, interferes with the single mood by introducing not only the social mixtures deplored by Sidney, the mingle of kings and clowns, but also the mixture of tones, the mingle of hornpipes and funerals which more Aristotelian kinds of drama will not tolerate.

Now this multiplicity of plot and character and stage space, of times and tones and conditions—the mixture of genres, also, which produces the hybrids and crossbreeds catalogued by Polonius [from *Hamlet*]—is reflected in the verbal medium. Greek tragedy utilizes its hexameters . . . and punctuates the dialogue at regular intervals with choric odes. French neoclassic drama adheres with singleminded fierceness to the Alexandrine couplet. Ibsen, once past his youthful days of experiment with poetic drama, adopts a realistic prose as his standard idiom. But in the Elizabethan drama every kind of verbal style jostles every other. We have both prose and verse: a prose ranging from the most unkempt and colloquial to the most loftily ceremonial, from the most syntactically disordered to the most artfully symmetrical, and a verse which, along with the staple, blank verse, includes rhymed pentameter couplets, octosyllabic couplets, doggerel couplets, lyric and stanzaic and strophic forms, all combined and recombined in endless permutation—as, for example, in Shakespeare's *A Midsummer Night's Dream,* with the blank verse of Theseus and Hippolyta, the pentameter couplets of the lovers, the octosyllabic couplets of Robin Goodfellow, the songs and lullabies of the attendant faeries, the clownish prose of Bottom and his associates, and the even more clownish stanzaic verses they recite in their playlet of Pyramus and Thisbe.

Elizabethan dramatic language, moreover, runs heavily to wordplay, and more particularly, to puns. Puns involve precisely the exploiting of the mutiplicities in language, the unlocking of two or more meanings imprisoned in a single word. One could compile a lexicon of words that nearly always contain a punning sense in Elizabethan dramatic dialogue—like crown, royal, noble, angel, cross, face, grace, kind—and a goodly number also that along with the explicator of ambiguity, [English critic and poet] William Empson, we would designate as complex—like blood, sense, honest, or fool—which cover a range of meanings too wide to be easily schematized. The verbal medium is a kind of three-piled texture, and the dramatists are constantly seeking to unravel the weave, to hold the words up to the light so as to discover the strands of sense woven into them. Racine, by contrast, works with a notoriously tiny vocabulary, where the words sometimes acquire a high expressive charge, and attain the status of symbols, but never the unstable, skittish, multiform identities of their Elizabethan counterparts. In this sphere as in others, where the non-Elizabethan drama presses toward clarity and economy, the Elizabethans long for total inclusiveness. They try to jam a whole linguistic universe into a word or a phrase or a line, bewildering us with the treasures they have to offer, until we are tempted to follow [twentieth-century critic] Molly Maureen Mahood's advice, who, after distinguishing four equally valid possible readings of a line in Shakespeare's *Romeo and Juliet,* ends by recommending that with "cormorant delight" we simply "swallow the lot." The Elizabethan mode, in all of its manifestations, approaches surfeit, prompting not only cormorant appetites like Miss Mahood's but also fastidious shrinkings like that of [American critic and author] Edmund Wilson, who complained of Jonson's *Bartholomew Fair* that there is in it "so much too much of everything that the whole thing becomes rather a wallow of which the Pig-woman and her pigs are all too truly the symbol."

As a final consideration one might mention the dialectical and open-ended nature of Elizabethan drama, as expounded by [twentieth-century] critics like Norman Rabkin, who sees Shakespeare's plays as marked by "complementarity"—which is to say that they are multiple in meaning and irreducible to a single formulable argument. Shakespeare, in this view—and, I would add, often the other Elizabethans as well—does not encourage us to assign a final interpretation to the events of his plots, does not opt for one among two or more conflicting points of view, but presents them all pitted against each other, each with its own irrefutable force and weight, requiring us to hold them in suspension in our minds as unresolved simultaneities.

CHAPTER 2

Elizabethan Drama as a Reflection of Elizabethan Society

Elizabethan Drama

Shakespeare's Portrayal of the Elizabethan Family

Marianne Novy

In the following essay, Marianne Novy examines historian Lawrence Stone's claim that the Elizabethan family is characterized by emotional distance. Although some historians have argued against Stone's conclusion, Novy contends that familial relationships in William Shakespeare's plays written during the Elizabethan era are in fact marked by emotional detachment and a struggle to remain dispassionate. According to Novy, while Stone's hypothesis may not be historically accurate, it does bring to light a theme that is important to Elizabethan literature. Novy is a professor of English at the University of Pittsburgh. She has written or edited several books on Shakespeare, including *Love's Argument: Gender Relations in Shakespeare.*

One of the most startling ideas in historian Lawrence Stone's *The Family, Sex, and Marriage in England 1500–1800* is the claim that most people in sixteenth- and early seventeenth-century England "found it very difficult to establish close emotional ties to any other person." As he reconstructs it, the Elizabethan family was characterized by "distance, manipulation, and deference." Stone may overstate his case, but evidence suggests that he is onto something. Some of his harshest critics, like Alan Macfarlane and Randolph Trumbach, point to similar cultural traits in the England they describe in their own work, though they differ with him about origin, time span, and degree. It seems that the Elizabethan aristocracy and middle class strove at least to appear in control of their emotional attachments, though the cost might be suspicion and loneliness.

Excerpted from "Shakespeare and Emotional Distance in the Elizabethan Family," by Marianne Novy, *Theatre Journal*, October 1981, pp. 316–25; ©1981, The Johns Hopkins University Press. Reprinted by permission of The Johns Hopkins University Press. (Footnotes in the original have been omitted in this reprint.)

The world Stone recreates and the world William Shake-speare creates are in sharp contrast. Plays characterized by the "psychic numbing" Stone attributes to Elizabethan society could never have held the stage for centuries, but beyond this, as C.L. Barber has noted, "Shakespeare's art is distinguished by the intensity of its investment in the human family." Are Shakespeare's plays evidence that Stone must be wrong about the Elizabethans? Or was Shakespeare simply ahead of his time in his portrayal of the family? Or is there another kind of relationship between Stone's picture and Shakespeare's?

LAWRENCE STONE'S DEPICTION OF ELIZABETHAN SOCIETY

The relationship I am proposing is not a photographic like-ness. It is not enough to say that the warm affectionate fam-ilies in Shakespeare show that Stone is wrong, or that cold families prove him right. Rather, I would suggest that Stone has identified a cultural ideal of Elizabethan society that generates conflicts pervasive in Shakespeare's plays.

According to Stone, most Elizabethan aristocrats were egocentric. Letters of advice from father to son, a popular genre among the landed classes, "normally express a thor-oughly pessimistic view of human nature, full of canny and worldly-wise hints about how to conduct personal relations which leave little room for generosity, faith, hope, or char-ity." Diaries, correspondence, and legal records from the fif-teenth to the seventeenth centuries show an extraordinary amount of casual violence at all levels of society.

The mortality rate for all ages and classes was high (infant mortality did not drop significantly until 1750) and Stone em-phasizes practices that can be viewed as treating people as easily replaceable. Aristocrats often used marriage to gain money or power, and remarriage was frequent. Upper-class children were sent out to a succession of wet nurses (who were separated from the children they had borne) and chil-dren of all classes lived apart from their parents for the years that they were in fosterage or apprenticeship.

What these facts meant emotionally is not easy to say, and some of the evidence could be interpreted differently. If aris-tocratic fathers told sons not to trust anyone, perhaps sons provoked the advice by trusting people. If sermons warned parents not to love their children too much, and threatened that God might take away a child whose parents were too fond, some parents must have grieved intensely for their children; Stone himself suggests that apparent coldness may have been a defense against the constant possibility of emotional bereavement. He notes too that some people married for emotional reasons, and that Reformation theology and practice placed more emphasis on companionship and love in marriage than had pre-Reformation Catholicism.

Nevertheless, Stone's work and that of other historians suggest that there was an ideal personality type valued by many Elizabethans—an ideal that on one hand kept feelings of attachment and grief under strict control but on the other was more ready to express feelings of anger. . . .

Family Bonds in Shakespeare's Tragedies

If establishing or admitting emotional ties was difficult for many in Shakespeare's audience partly because of their ideals of control, this ambivalence may have contributed to the appeal of his plays. In the tragedies, the cost of either denying or affirming connections can be mortal; in the comedies, more connections succeed. But in the background of both genres are distances—literal and psychological—between parents and children, and disguises—literal and psychological—that attempt control and dramatize the difficulties of trusting and understanding. . . .

King Lear . . . is about conflicts between distance and emotion in relations between parent and child. Lear cannot freely express his love for Cordelia, but must set up his intended gift as a reward for her performance in a contest he controls, and then disowns her for insisting on her autonomy and not playing her part properly. While his other daughters treat him cruelly, he strives to control himself and deny his emotional vulnerability; but these attempts break down in his madness. Only Cordelia can save him, and he breaks down again when she is lost forever; but in Lear's death, as he strains again for a word from her, it is clear they are inevitably bound to each other. With similar lack of insight, Gloucester dismisses Edmund with "He hath been out nine year, and away he shall again" (I. i. 31–2), and then doubts Edgar's love on the flimsiest of evidence manufactured by Edmund; he underestimates the anger of the one and the love of the other and the impact that both will have on his life. Edgar, his identity disguised, cares for his father in the blindness that his brother helped to cause. When Edgar reveals himself, Gloucester dies of mingled grief and joy, like Lear showing in his death the strength of his connection to his child.

In one sense, Hamlet's initial manner is already an acknowledgment of his bond to his family; his mourning is an attempt to maintain the tie to the father that death has removed. But in this attempt to cling to his father he seems distant from his mother, and we can trace something of an analogous pattern to the one we have seen in . . . *Lear.* At first Hamlet speaks to his mother only in laconic irony—"Ay, madam, it is common" (I. ii. 74). But later when he speaks to her in her room, it becomes clear how much anger underlies this distance, and how much longing for love underlies the anger.

However, the relevance to *Hamlet* of the emotional distance Stone has described in Elizabethan England is even clearer if we look at the larger structure of the play. *Hamlet* is built around a conflict between an unfeeling society and a hero with strong feelings, which he tries to control—a conflict that parallels both the conflicts I postulated for Elizabethan England—the internal one between defenses and emotions and the external one between cooler and more emotional people. The mood of the Danish court sounds much like that of the suspicious Elizabethan court—even Polonius's advice resembles that of the many cynical fathers found by Stone. Hamlet must live among detached, manipulative, and suspicious people, and he defends himself from them partly by trying to mask his emotional intensity with emotional distance. He speaks enigmatically from the very beginning—"A little more than kin and less than kind" (I. ii. 65)—and puts on a more elaborate antic disposition after the ghost's revelation widens the gap between him and the rest of the court. He can trust Horatio, but no one else, and it is only after Ophelia's death that he can admit his love for her.

When trust is created in the tragedies, it is a precarious achievement in a perilous world. Othello's relationship with Desdemona breaks down in the context of threats analogous to those Stone suggests—distrust resulting from ideals of emotional control. Living down the stereotype of the passionate African and the unease of the exile, he too is a hero of strong feelings he strives to control. Throughout, the cynical and manipulative worldview has its spokesman in Iago. Emotionally detached from his own wife, he can influence Othello partly because of the basic sense of insecurity and distance which makes it difficult for Othello to believe in the initial success of his love, and partly because of Othello's ideals of coolness. From the beginning he has denied the presence of "heat" or "young affects" in his love. When his jealousy shows him his passionate attachment to Desdemona, he believes it is alien to his true character and plans to kill her to restore his self-control: "I'll not expostulate with her, lest her body and beauty unprovide my mind again" (IV. i. 200–2). When he discovers her fidelity, only his own death can restore that control, and his death is equally an attempt to reaffirm their relationship.

EMOTIONAL CONNECTIONS IN COMEDIES

In the comedies, the conflicts between emotional distance and control do not require death for their resolution. Thus the distance between parent and child is often presented largely as geographic distance and physical disguise. Parent-child separation and parent-child rejection are kept apart (rather than being combined as they are in *Othello* and *Lear*). In *The Comedy of Errors,* Antipholus of Ephesus speaks movingly of his separation from his parents, caused by the romance plot conventions of tempest and shipwreck. Here, and in the romances as well, such externally enforced family separation could dramatize the frequent separation of Elizabethan families by death and standard child-rearing practices. Feeling separation as rejection probably alternated with feeling it as beyond human control like tempest and shipwreck. The reticence that the Antipholus brothers keep in their reunion—they never speak directly to each other—may show that the ideal of emotional control continues its claims even at the happy ending. At the corresponding point, the Menachmi twins of Shakespeare's source speak to each other with feeling, and we might expect even more eloquence at the father-son reunion not found in the source, but we do not get it. This inarticulacy allows the actors to fill in with gestures, of course, and the audience with imagination; nevertheless it is interesting that it is the mother who has almost all the words of joy at the resolution, and that her imagery turns on childbirth:

> Thirty-three years have I but gone in travail
> Of you, my sons; and till this present hour
> My heavy burden ne'er delivered.

> [V. i. 402–4]

The disguises in Shakespeare's comedies can be related to emotional distance in a number of ways. The self-control that masculine disguise imposes on women is an analogue of the control that the masculine ideal imposes on men; the disguise suggests, too, that the women may share in that ideal of control. Rosalind begins *As You Like It* grieving for her banished father, but when she meets him she does not at once reveal the identity behind her disguise. "He asked me of what parentage I was. I told him, of as good as he; so he laughed and let me go" (III. iv. 33–4). For all of her warmth, Rosalind maintains some freedom and distance from her father until the last scene. But unlike Edgar's analogous delay in revealing himself, this one has no mortal consequences.

For the lovers in the comedies, disguise can dramatize the difficulties of establishing emotional connections, although it also fosters such connections by giving less risky ones time to develop. Rosalind's disguise may express ambivalence about abandoning herself to her love for Orlando; in many of the comedies, the characters' inability to see through disguise suggests their mixed feelings about forming close ties. Sherman Hawkins has noted the internal obstacles to love in what he calls the comedies of the closed world *(Comedy of Errors, Taming of the Shrew, Love's Labour's Lost, Much Ado About Nothing* and *Twelfth Night);* Orlando's initial inability to speak to Rosalind suggests an internal obstacle in him as well. Proteus, Berowne, Bassanio, Orlando, Claudio, and Orsino[1] all make mistakes about the identity of the women they finally marry. These mistakes, and analogous mistakes made by Phebe and Olivia,[2] are, in part, dramatic images of the postures of emotional distance that can remain even when falling in love; many of these characters are comically self-centered or fascinated with an idealized image—often unattainable—more than with a human being. Often the degree to which the characters grow is open to question, and the conclusion relies primarily on the literal removal of disguise for the sense of overcoming barriers to relationship. . . .

EMOTIONAL CONTROL AND GENDER DIFFERENCES

Emotional control was more clearly an ideal for men than for women in Elizabethan society. Stone gives largely unexplored

---

1. from the following plays, in order: *Two Gentleman of Verona, Love's Labour's Lost, The Merchant of Venice, As You Like It, Much Ado About Nothing,* and *Twelfth Night*
2. from *As You Like It* and *Twelfth Night,* respectively

hints that patterns and norms of emotional warmth differed
for males and females. The parents quoted as sounding distant from children are mostly fathers; furthermore, Stone sees
fathers as colder to daughters than to sons, more likely to consider daughters as only a drain on their money. He also provides some evidence that women often wanted more emotional involvement in marriage than did men. In this context,
the emphasis on distance and manipulativeness in father-son
advice letters looks different. Rather than expressing a general norm, it suggests an attempt to initiate the son into standards of coldness required by the conventional adult male.

How much was this a conscious rejection of qualities associated with women? Popular thought often identified
women with passion and men with reason, with an emphasis on the necessary subordination of the first to the second;
since women, whether nurses or mothers, had primary responsibility for child-rearing, they were associated with
everyone's first discovery of emotions. Many documents
suggest that Elizabethan men were often suspicious of
women, and this suspicion may also be connected with suspicion of feelings of attachment in general.

More historical research needs to be done on how the
ideal of emotional distance in the Elizabethan family relates
to distrust of women and qualities associated with women—
how much it coalesces with emotional distance as a conventional ideal for Elizabethan men. In Shakespeare the connection is often explicit. His characters use language that
associates women with expressions of emotional attachment; such language is especially frequent in bereavement.
Laertes says of his tears for Ophelia's death, "When these are
gone,/The woman will be out" (IV. vii. 187–8). When Sebastian [from *Twelfth Night*] thinks his sister Viola is dead, he
says, "I am yet so near the manners of my mother that, upon
the least occasion more, mine eyes will tell tales of me" (II. i.
35–7), and Claudius censures Hamlet's mourning by saying
"'Tis unmanly grief" (I. ii. 94). When Lear struggles to deny
the pain he feels at his daughters' rejection, he cries, "O, how
this mother swells up toward my heart! /Hysterica passio,
down, thou climbing sorrow" (II. iv. 54–5). Later he prays

> Touch me with noble anger,
> And let not women's weapons, water drops,
> Stain my man's cheeks.
>
> [II. iv. 271–3]

This pattern of associations often goes beyond words. Most of the rejections of children are rejections of daughters by fathers. Let us recall Leonato and Hero, Old Capulet and Juliet, Brabantio and Desdemona, Cymbeline and Imogen.[3] Furthermore, fathers' rejections of daughters, like husbands' rejections of wives, usually result from suspicion of female sexuality—in one case (Perdita [from *The Winter's Tale*]) the daughter is thought to be conceived adulterously, in the others, the fathers object to their daughters' wishes, real or apparent, to love men other than their fathers or their fathers' choices. By contrast, neither mothers nor fathers reject sons because of their sexual behavior. And on the other hand, verbal attacks on a mother's sexuality may suddenly appear in any threat of rejection from the family, even if the mother herself never appears in the play. Lear says to Regan: "I would divorce me from thy mother's tomb/ Sepulch'ring an adult'ress" (II. iv. 126–7), and Isabella to Claudio: "Heaven shield my mother played my father fair, /For such a warpèd slip of wilderness/Never issued from his blood" (III. i. 141–3).[4]

In general, attempts at self-control that inhibit relationships are more central to Shakespeare's male characters than to his female ones. This does not mean that all the women are warm and compassionate while all the men are cold and controlled, as the passage from Isabella's tirade should remind us; but the characters often speak as if such qualities have each an appropriate sex. Almost all Shakespearean tragic heroes and several heroes in the romances and problem plays distrust both female characters and qualities in themselves that they consider female. Yet they do love those characters and possess those qualities. They ultimately find it necessary to express their emotions beyond the cold ideals of their society. They learn, like Lear, that they must weep. Thus the plays implicitly criticize the view of manhood as opposed to feeling. Occasionally the characters themselves hint at different ideals, as Macduff does in his bereavements when he answers "Dispute it like a man" with "I shall do so; / but I must also feel it as a man" (IV. iii. 220–1) [in *Macbeth*]. And in the romances a few of the men learn to reverse the disparagement of female characteristics, and can welcome family reunion with the imagery of child-

---

3. from the following plays, in order: *Much Ado About Nothing, Romeo and Juliet, Othello,* and *Cymbeline*   4. from *King Lear* and *Measure for Measure*, respectively

birth that in *The Comedy of Errors* only a woman could use: Cymbeline says, on finding his children again, "O, what am I? / A mother to the birth of three? Ne'er mother / Rejoiced deliverance more" (V. v. 368–70).

Much of this could be observed by critics whose interest is not primarily historical. But much of the new social history shows that conflicting trends in marriage and the family are not simply a twentieth-century imposition on Shakespeare; it provides a cautionary note for any critic who would look for a psychopathology for Shakespeare in isolation from his society. Stone's view of Elizabethan England is one-sided, as other historians have shown, but he does help us see one side of a conflict important in Shakespeare's plays.

Puritanism and Its Impact on the Depiction of Women in Elizabethan Drama

Juliet Dusinberre

The reign of Queen Elizabeth I witnessed the growth of Puritanism, an offshoot of English Protestantism that encouraged individualism. In relation to the role of women in Elizabethan society, Puritanism argued that women were entitled to a certain level of independence and should not be required to obey an unethical husband. These views are exemplified in many Elizabethan plays, including William Shakespeare's *Othello* and *Hamlet,* which depict women struggling for freedom and the right to follow their conscience. Juliet Dusinberre is a professor of English at Cambridge University's Girton College. She is the author of *Shakespeare and the Nature of Women,* from which this essay is excerpted.

In the sixteenth century the idea that women had consciences which might operate independently from men's, might even judge and oppose the male conscience, was revolutionary. Even in Elizabethan drama there are vestiges of the medieval schoolmen's debate about whether women had souls. Launce in William Shakespeare's *The Two Gentlemen of Verona* makes his left shoe stand for his mother because 'it hath the worser sole.' Yet the reformers declared God to be no respecter of sexes, 'for in Christ,' said the Humanist[1] Henricus Cornelius Agrippa, 'Neither Male nor Female, but a new creature is accepted.' He argued, in a passage which re-

---

1. Humanism is a literary and philosophical movement that emphasizes human values and capabilities.

Excerpted from *Shakespeare and the Nature of Women,* by Juliet Dusinberre. Copyright ©1975 by Juliet Dusinberre. Reprinted with permission from St. Martin's Press, LLC.

calls [English scholar Thomas] More's claim for women's spiritual equality in his letter to his daughters' tutor, Gunnell, that 'it is manifest that the difference of the Sexes consists only in the different Scituation of the parts of the Body, which the office of generation did necessarily require. But certain it is, he gave one and the same indifferent soule to Male and Female.' When the Protestants supported the rights of the individual conscience against the authority of the Church, they created the conditions of support for the rights of individual women against the men in authority over them. If God created a partnership in Eden, He must have allowed freedom of conscience to both halves.

The Puritans had an interest in urging freedom of conscience for women in that the Puritan sects boasted a considerable female membership, perhaps for the general reason that women tend to be active in minority groups because they can exert more influence as individuals on a small new organisation than on a big one with traditional male dominance. More specifically the Puritan ideology backed women in a venture which was educative, politically orientated, and feminist in its implementation. Meetings of sects and Puritan lectures gave women a context outside the home. The sects admitted women on equal terms with men, allowed them to minister, and gave them an equal share in the government of the sect. They provided a sphere in which a woman might be independent of her husband. The more radical sects like the Anabaptists, the Brownists or the Family of Love[2]—satirised in Thomas Middleton's play [*The Family of Love*]—held that a woman had no marital obligations to an unbelieving husband. In cases of difference the judge was her own conscience, and in cases of the antagonistic claims of husband and sect, her first loyalty should be to the sect. John Knox[3] in Geneva gathered round him a community which included emigré women like Anne Locke who had fled the rule of an unregenerate husband. Katherine Chidley, who was to be one of the most active leaders of the Levellers,[4] and who wrote a pioneering pamphlet on the

2. The Anabaptists were a sixteenth-century religious sect that was against infant baptism, arguing that baptism was only appropriate for believers. The Brownists were a separatist group named for clergyman Robert Browne; separatists were Christians who withdrew from the Church of England and sought freedom from church authority. The Family of Love, or Familists, was a radical religious sect that believed in social equality and rejected institutionalized religion.   3. John Knox founded Scottish Presbyterianism. He went into exile in Geneva, Switzerland, after the accession of England's Queen Mary, a Catholic.   4. The Levellers were a popular movement that began in England during the mid-seventeenth century and supported democratic self-government.

right of women to independence of conscience, left her husband, and, with her son, started a new Brownist community in Bury, Suffolk. Women protested so militantly against the suppression of Puritan preachers that they went to prison for their activities. Puritanism, which idealised the divine union of man and wife, operated, at least on the sectarian level, in a way which made women more conscious of their separateness from their husbands. Democracy develops out of a man's sense of an identity distinct from his relation to those who rule him, through which he can confront that rule. The Puritan sects offered women an identity apart from their husbands, which made it possible for them to challenge their husbands' authority. . . .

DRAMATISTS' PORTRAYALS OF WOMEN'S FREEDOM

The dramatists reacted in three main ways to the controversy about freedom of conscience for women. In the first place, their satire on the sects took the form of demonstrating the licence of women sectarians as the most inflammatory area for arousing general opposition to sectarianism. They concentrated on the sects' annexing of property—both financial and sexual—through their women members, on their encouragement of mental insubordination, and on their motley class elements. The sects were predominantly lower-class in membership and when Quarlous in Ben Jonson's *Bartholomew Fair* scoffs at the 'good labourers and painful eaters' class antagonism is as strong, if not stronger, than religious feeling. In *The Family of Love* Dryfat describes the sect as

> a crew of narrow-ruffed, strait-laced, yet loose-bodied dames, with a rout of omnium-gatherums, assembled by the title of the Family of Love: which, master doctor, if they be not punished and suppressed by our club-law, each man's copyhold will become freehold, specialities will turn to generalities. . . . Their wives, the only ornaments of their houses, and of all their wares, goods, and chattel[s], the chief moveables, will be made common.

The idea of wives in common, the complaint of the husband in George Chapman's *An Humorous Day's Mirth* of his sectarian wife, that 'every man for her sake is a Puritan,' was as distasteful to the middle-class family man as the picture of the wife embezzling his money to support the sect which Truewit evokes for Morose in Jonson's *Epicoene*. The dramatists unerringly touched the tender areas of feeling about the sects, displaying witty and incorrigible women sectarians evading their husbands' control. Even Mrs Purge in *The Family of Love* eludes her husband's accusation that he has cuckolded himself, swearing, with Falstaffian[5] facility, that she knew him all along, and turning aside his plea that she attend the sect no more with the counter-argument of freedom of conscience:

> Truly, husband, my love must be free still to God's creatures:
> yea, nevertheless, preserving you still as the head of my body,
> I will do as the spirit shall enable me.

Katherine Chidley might have said the same to her husband before she left.

OBEDIENCE AND REBELLION

Secondly, the dramatists focused on situations in which the wife's conscience took a different course from her husband's. The Puritans believed that a man must adhere to ethical standards with which his wife could identify; if he failed to do so, she had the right to disavow his authority. 'The husband saith, that his wife must obey him because he is her better, therefore if he let her be better than himselfe, he seemes to free her from obedience, and binde himselfe to obay her.'[6] Emilia in Shakespeare's *Othello* is not alone in repudiating the rule of a husband inferior to her in virtue. Staring in horror at Iago disfigured by her new knowledge of him, she defies his command for her silence: ''Tis proper I obey him, but not now.' A husband's villainy annuls his wife's duty to him. Middleton's Thomasine in *Michaelmas Term*, watching her husband ruining another man, exclaims: 'Why am I wife to him that is no man?' In Shakespeare's *The Winter's Tale* Leontes responds to Paulina's curses on his cruelty to Hermione by turning to her husband: 'What! canst not rule her?' The retort comes not from a wife, but from an individual capable of distinguishing good and evil without the intervention of a third party:

> From all dishonesty he can: in this—
> Unless he take the course that you have done,
> Commit me for committing honour—trust it,
> He shall not rule me.

Women can be for God only, as well as men.

---

5. Sir John Falstaff is one of Shakespeare's most popular comic characters, present in *Henry IV, Parts I and II* and *The Merry Wives of Windsor.*   6. Henry Smith, *A Preparative to Marriage*, 1591. Published by W.J. Johnson: Norwood, NJ, 1975.

In some women obedience itself may have the impact of defiance, where rebellion would put the wife on the same level morally as her corrupted husband. When Othello strikes Desdemona as though she were his whore, her submission passes judgement on him more tellingly than a retaliation which would draw her into an ethical universe which settled moral issues with physical violence. Marriage on these terms is no better than a tavern brawl, the forays between Jonson's Cob and Tib in *Every Man In His Humour* where the wife adopts Henry Smith's reversal of roles, and agrees to take Cob back into favour only as 'my louing, and obedient husband.' Desdemona's obedience bespeaks a clear conscience; her behaviour is independent of her husband's judgement of her. Lodovico marvels: 'Truly an obedient lady.' Othello's scorn fails to touch her, because her submission separates her from the confines of his moral vision:

> Sir, she can turn, and turn, and yet go on,
> And turn again, and she can weep, sir, weep;
> And she's obedient, as you say, obedient;
> Very obedient. Proceed you in your tears.

His unkindness cannot taint her goodness because its existence is not dependent on his favour. Othello's remorse scalds him the more for his wife's refusal to accuse him:

> When we shall meet at compt,
> This look of thine will hurl my soul from heaven,
> And fiends will snatch at it.

In Shakespeare's *Cymbeline* Imogen's determination to obey Posthumus when she learns his desire for her death exposes his ignobility more devastatingly than defiance could: she prepares to kill herself:

> And thou, Posthumus, thou that didst set up
> My disobedience 'gainst the king my father,
> And make me put into contempt the suits
> Of princely fellows, shall hereafter find
> It is no act of common passage, but
> A strain of rareness.

In both women submission is not the negative acquiescence of an indolent conscience but a mark of rareness which spots rebellion with commonness.

INDEPENDENT WOMEN

Thirdly, the Puritan debate about freedom of conscience made the dramatists interested in women on their own. Eliz-

MUTUAL RESPECT IN *THE TAMING OF THE SHREW*

One of the most debated speeches in Shakespeare's plays is at the end of The Taming of the Shrew, *when Kate explains the need for wifely obedience. Scholars have argued over whether Kate's words should be taken at face value. In her book* Shakespeare and His Social Context: Essays in Osmotic Knowledge and Literary Interpretation, *Margaret Loftus Ranald contends that through the characters of Kate and her husband Petruchio, Shakespeare is in fact showing how the ideal marriage is based on mutual respect. Ranald likens the relationship to that of a falconer and his falcon (or haggard)—the falcon must learn to be obedient but its hunting instinct cannot be broken.*

Kate's set speech on wifely duties (V. ii. 140–184) has frequently been misunderstood and often misplayed. Sometimes it is performed too obsequiously, and sometimes too ironically, with a too broad wink at the end, but more frequently it has been completely misread. What it celebrates is a mutual agreement, a bargain in terms of separation of powers. The husband is legally the head of the wife as her lord, keeper, king, and governor, but he also has duties. He must provide for his family, and as prince in his own household, he should rule its members with justice and loving kindness rather than cruelty and injustice. In return, the wife too has duties, basically those of "love, fair looks, and true obedience" (l. 158). She owes her husband the same "duty as the subject owes the prince" (l. 160). She must submit to his "honest will" (l. 163), and not rebel against his reasonable demands. This situation seems to indicate a mutuality of aims and a tolerance of personal differences.

The key words of the speech are "true obedience" and "honest will." Neither of these concepts of behavior indicates force or tyranny, but rather mutual respect, trust, tolerance, and understanding. . . .

Through the careful equation of the taming of a wife with the "reclaiming" of a haggard, Shakespeare has conveyed the ideal matrimonial situation. Both keeper and falcon, husband and wife, have their own areas of superiority, but when both work together at a given hunting task they are incomparable. Each needs the other, and each recognizes the necessity of love and obedience on the part of the one, and consideration and trust on the part of the other. Each has duties and both have rights.

Margaret Loftus Ranald, *Shakespeare and His Social Context: Essays in Osmotic Knowledge and Literary Interpretation.* New York: AMS Press, 1987.

abethan drama has no Antigones.[7] Surprisingly, in an age ob-
sessed with the individual conscience, there are no plays
about women vowed to great causes, unless one counts
Dorothea, the Christian heroine of Philip Massinger's particularly vile play about decadent Rome, *The Virgin Martyr.*
The women of the political world—the Duchess of Malfi,[8]
Katherine in Shakespeare's *Henry VIII,* even Margaret in
Shakespeare's *Henry VI* plays and Shakespeare's *Richard
III*—are smaller, more domestic figures than Sophocles'
heroine. The choices open to their consciences are more
confused: they are more captive in the fact of womanhood
and more impotent. The grand gesture of tragedy is less
available to them than it is to a character like [seventeenth-
century French dramatist Jean] Racine's Bérénice. Shakespeare's theatre offers instead a consistent probing of the reactions of women to isolation in a society which has never
allowed them independence from men either physically or
spiritually. The struggle is not about issues—the gods and the
State—it is about what [twentieth-century writer] Virginia
Woolf called 'The Angel in the House,' the male idea of womanhood. The dramatists took the concept of a man's domin-
ion over his wife and daughters, and explored what it was
like to be a woman under these conditions. The interplay between breaking free and submitting to the male world's view
of women is inseparable from the characters of women as
disparate as [from Shakespeare's *King Lear*] Goneril, Helena
in Shakespeare's *All's Well That Ends Well,* Shakespeare's
Portia in *The Merchant of Venice,* Lady Macbeth, or Vittoria in
Webster's *The White Devil.* Tragedy is supposed to deal with
the isolation of the human spirit, and one of the reasons for
the Elizabethan and Jacobean preoccupation with heroines
is that that isolation is more terrible in a being conditioned to
dependence on men. Lady Macbeth, forever recreating in her
sleep-walking the inception of her separateness from her
husband, still reaches for his hand. But Shakespeare's comedies evince the same fascination with women on their own,
from the solitary sorrow of Julia in *The Two Gentlemen of
Verona,* watching her lover court another woman, to Viola
communing with her disguised self, 'How will this fadge?' [in

7. In Greek legend, Antigone is one of Oedipus' daughters. After her brothers Eteocles
and Polynices kill each other, the king of Thebes forbids the burial of the rebel Polynices. Antigone disobeys the order and is ultimately condemned to death. The Greek
drama *Antigone* by Sophocles depicts this story.   8. from the John Webster play of the
same name

Twelfth Night] to Helena and Hermia, alternately exiled from the trio of competing lovers in *A Midsummer Night's Dream.*

Antigone's breeding has not quenched the fire of independence in her; her conscience is not a female one but a human one. In late Elizabethan drama the struggle for women is to be human in a world which declares them only female. The effect of Puritanism on the drama was to excite interest in what a woman's conscience would dictate to her if she were freed from subjection to the male conscience. Hamlet battles to make his mother independent of Claudius, taunting her with the possibility of breach of confidence:

> 'Twere good you let him know,
> For who that's but a queen, fair, sober, wise,
> Would from a paddock, from a bat, a gib,
> Such dear concernings hide?

Freedom of conscience for women was still a new concept. Women had not been educated to form independent moral judgements. The dramatists asked themselves how the female conscience would work, given the authoritarian conditions of its nurture, or rather non-nurture. [Eighteenth-century feminist] Mary Wollstonecraft urged that 'some degree of liberty of mind is necessary even to form the person.' Polonius dispatches his son to the university to sow his wild oats, to learn through his errors how to be true to himself, and thus to other men. But his daughter must not rely on her own judgement. Her conviction of Hamlet's sincerity arouses contempt: 'Affection, pooh! you speak like a green girl / Unsifted in such perilous circumstance.' He advises her to

> think yourself a baby
> That you have ta'en these tenders for true pay
> Which are not sterling.

Laertes expects Ophelia to heed his counsel that 'best safety lies in fear.' Her whole education is geared to relying on other people's judgements, and to placing chastity and the reputation for chastity above even the virtue of truthfulness. Ophelia has no chance to develop an independent conscience of her own, so stifled is she by the authority of the male world. The consequence is, that being false to herself, allowing herself to acquiesce in the deception by which her father and the king overhear her conversation with Hamlet, she is inevitably false to Hamlet. His 'Get thee to a nunnery' mocks a morality which thinks chastity compatible with hypocrisy. Under this tutelage women are degraded into creatures with no moral sense of their own, who have to be incarcerated in nunneries to keep them virtuous. Polonius allows Ophelia no identity independent of his rule, a condition which makes her incapable of coping with a world in which he has no part—the world of her relation to Hamlet. Her reason has not been educated to exercise itself without his guidance: 'Lord, we know what we are, but know not what we may be.' When Claudius laments 'poor Ophelia / Divided from herself and her fair judgment,' the irony lies in the fact that she was never allowed to have any judgement.

Mary Wollstonecraft's cynicism about the traditional attitude that 'with respect to the female character, obedience is the grand lesson which ought to be impressed with unrelenting vigour,' was anticipated by sixteenth-century Humanists when they argued that women need liberty to develop into people. Subjection, pointed out Agrippa, is self-perpetuating in women because:

> A woman by and by as soon as she is borne, and from the first beginning of her years is detained in sloth at home, and as uncapable of another Province, she is permitted to think of nothing besides her Needle or the like, when afterwards she reacheth to ripenesse of age, she is delivered up to the jealous rule of her husband, or else shut up in the perpetual Bridewell of Nuns.

In Jonson's *Every Man In His Humour* Mrs Kitely suffers the jealous rule of a husband, where the treatment of Young Knowell recognises different principles. Knowell is unwilling to compel his son to virtue, preferring to give him his head to learn the meaning of virtue rather than its rules. Justice Clement reinforces his view: 'Your sonne is old inough, to gouerne himselfe: let him runne his course, it's the onely way to make him a stay'd man.' The play ends, like Shakespeare's *The Merry Wives of Windsor,* with the husband learning that what is sauce for the gander is sauce for the goose, and that a wife is more likely to be virtuous if trusted to be so than if compelled to be so, a compulsion which any woman of wit will evade. For both sexes, liberty is the soil in which conscience takes root. To preach freedom of conscience for women demanded recognition of their need for freedom from male authority.

Othello Questions Some Elizabethan Racial Stereotypes

Rudolph Shaw

Elizabethans viewed black Africans with a mixture of fascination and fear. As Rudolph Shaw points out in the following essay, because of their dark skin and their non-Christian heritage, blacks were thought to be associated with the devil. Blacks were subject to much unjust stereotyping and characterized as wicked and beastly in dramas and other forms of popular culture. In William Shakespeare's *Othello*, the title character, a black Moor, is frequently maligned and judged by other characters because of his skin color. However, as Shaw notes, Shakespeare refuses to accede to the stereotypes, making Othello a complex individual whose failures are the result of human weaknesses and not perceived racial flaws. Shaw is a Guyanese actor with a doctorate in educational theater and dramatherapy.

Genetic differences among humans have always been a source of prejudice, discontent, and other social evils; enough to make a beautiful swan seem like an ugly duckling. Interracial marriages are often frowned upon in some societies, and a great fascination exists for interracial marriage of the black and white combination. It transcends the realm of "real" love and enters the zone of passion for the forbidden fruit of the opposite skin color. Even in our contemporary learned societies, stereotypical names are often attached to such couples—in Spain it is "leche y chocolate" (milk and chocolate), in the United States of America it is "Jungle Fever" from the popular movie on the topic. Did Elizabethans refer to such couples as "Othello and Desdemona"? Quite possibly: and blamed such labelling on

Reprinted by permission of Transaction Publishers from "*Othello* and Race Relations in Elizabethan England," by Rudolph Shaw, *Journal of African American Men*, Summer 1995. Copyright ©1995 by Transaction Publishers; all rights reserved.

William Shakespeare's boldness to go beyond the "base alliance" (Given, 1899) of his peers in treating the topic of black and white relationships. "It is a bold thing to bring a coal-black Moor on the stage as the husband of a delicate, loving bride" (Given, 1899).

RACE RELATIONS IN EARLIER DRAMA

The Elizabethan audience had already seen several works dealing with race relationships in the popular horror plays like Shakespeare's *Titus Andronicus*. Plays that incorporated executions, murders, mutilations and rapes were part of the common dramatic fare of the Elizabethan Theater (Wright and La Mar, 1967). These plays represented the sensationalism Elizabethans loved in the theater. "The plays of the Roman dramatist Seneca were well known, and exerted a powerful influence on early Elizabethan drama . . . nothing could be too bloody and horrible for an Elizabethan audience" (Wright and La Mar, 1967). Mixed with this desire for blood and horror in the theater was the conventional wicked Moor character in the Elizabethan and earlier literature (Wright and La Mar, 1967). Setting the drama in Italy appealed to the hypnotic fascination which Englishmen held for Renaissance Italy. It is no surprise therefore that both Shakespearean plays, in which the question of racial difference plays an important part, are set in Venice (Salgado, 1985). It is also not surprising that the source of *Othello* was a short story from the *Hecatommithi*—"a collection of tales brought out in 1565 by an Italian named Giovanni Battista Giraldi (Cinthio)" (Wright and La Mar, 1956). The story comes from the part that deals with 'The Unfaithfulness or Husbands and Wives'. While the character of 'Disdemona' is mentioned in the original, there is no reference to Othello, and Shakespeare's source for the name remains obscure (Wright and La Mar, 1956).

One suggestion of the source of the character of Othello is the miracle or mystery plays.[1] In creating a Moor who was black in the face yet white and noble in the spirit, Shakespeare had the perfect character to astound and perplex the already bloodthirsty Elizabethan audiences. Indeed, aspects of this character were already evident in the "blackened faces

---

1. Miracle plays, also known as mystery plays, were medieval dramas that presented the lives of saints or biblical stories.

of the old religious miracle or mystery play which suggested the introduction of dark visages into the secular drama in the form of Moors" (Given, 1899). The mystery play therefore provided the source from which Shakespeare was able to find "a suggestion of the means by which to extenuate the marriage of a refined white woman with a black. His debt to the mystery is greater than to Cinthio" (Given, 1899).

Some critics have written that "there is little to indicate that Shakespeare or his contemporaries would have interpreted the union of Othello and Desdemona as a problem of mixed marriage" (Wright and La Mar, 1956), or that racial difference was a major interest. They state that to an Elizabethan, a Moor was a swarthy man and the interest in Moors persisted because of the stories of the Moors in Spain. Shakespeare merely took the appellation 'the Moor' from the Italian source, and such use of the exotic was quite appropriate at the time (Wright and La Mar, 1956). While this may be true, there are many subliminal and blatant references to indicate the tone of race relations at the time.

Elizabethan Perspectives on Africa

In addressing this issue, it may be prudent to examine the Elizabethan view of the New World. This was a period in which Englishmen had to face the fact that there were strange people in other parts of the world. The slave trade had already started, and the Elizabethan period was the heyday of colonialism. Many Africans were brought back to England as proof of their existence. The Elizabethans' knowledge of the continent and peoples of Africa was bountiful. Contrary beliefs "ignore the fact that among the published writings of English voyagers well before 1600, there were reports of contacts with West African kings like the king of Benin in 'Negro-land', and that in the pages of John Leo's book several such kingdoms in 'Negro-land' had been vividly described" (Jones, 1965). The most significant of these publications was Sir John Mandeville's *Mandeville's Travels*, which stimulated the appetite of fifteenth century England for information about the continent of Africa and its inhabitants. "Many of the commonest notions which were held about the continent by Elizabethans can be traced back to this book" (Jones, 1965). One of the interesting contributions of *"Mandeville's Travels* to the notions of Africa is his description of the inhabitants with his repeated references to

their colour, particularly when the colour was black"
(Jones, 1965). These references established an automatic association of Africa with blackness in the minds of Englishmen (Jones, 1965).

The English recognized that the best way to colonize the
New World was through the exportation of their language
and culture. This desire to teach the barbaric peoples of the
New World the 'right' language and culture was very evident
during the Elizabethan period. In 1599, Samuel Daniel
wrote a philosophical poem which culminated in a vision of
future possibilities (Greenblatt, 1990):

> And who in time knowes whither we may vent
> The treasure of our tongue, to what strange shores
> This gaine or our best glorie shal be sent
> T'inrich unknowing Nations with our stores?
> What worlds in th'yet unformed Occident
> May come refin'd with th'accents that are ours?

Here Daniel sees the New World as a vast rich field for the
plantation of the English language. To many Elizabethans,
people from the New World were culturally naked. "This illusion that the inhabitants of the New World are essentially
without a culture of their own is . . . remarkedly persistent,
even in the face of overwhelming contradictory evidence"
(Greenblatt, 1990). Gregorio Garcia conducted a massive
study (published in 1607) which linked the languages found
in the New World with that of the devil—"Satan had helped
the Indians to invent new tongues, thus impeding the labors
of Christian missionaries" (Greenblatt, 1990). This association of Indians with the devil parallels Elizabethan views of
Africans as well; and the reference linking Othello to witchcraft in the play comes from this stereotypical image of
Africans. When Iago speaks to Brabantio (Desdemona's father) about Othello, he refers to him as an ugly lascivious
beast; very much like the popular notions of the devil.
"Iago's language represents the popular image of Moors in a
grotesquely distorted light; . . . moving to the popular associations of black with hell," he urges Brabantio to make
haste before the devil makes him a grandfather (Jones,
1965). His language to Brabantio, "an old black ram/Is tup-
ping your white ewe" (*Othello* I. i. 88–89) is loaded with references to Othello as the devilish beast—in fact the devil
himself (Jones, 1965). This image is currently seen in a certain United Colors of Benetton store advertisement in Italy.

RACIAL INTOLERANCE IN ELIZABETHAN ENGLAND

Iago's description and references to Othello as the devil touch on the popular European fears of the peoples of the New World. European response to these strange people was often clouded and controlled by their response to the legendary Wild Man characters[2] of Medieval and Renaissance literature. This reaction incorporated a mingled attraction and revulsion, longing and hatred (Greenblatt, 1990). The peoples of the New World did not conform to the European views of morality, family life, political and other institutions, and the church; and this greatly disturbed the Europeans who observed them. Indeed, one argument against freeing slaves was that once given liberty, these "wild" people would return to a life of unstable families, wantonness and perversion (Greenblatt, 1990). Iago's references to Othello as an "erring barbarian" and "extravagant wheeling stranger" definitely reminded Elizabethans of the Wild Man legend (Greenblatt, 1990). Also Roderigo's reference to Othello as "a lascivious Moor" in Act I. i, is an instant reminder to Elizabethans of the popular beliefs concerning the sexual promiscuity of Moors. Therefore, Othello is presented as a stereotypical black man by his peers, despite his acculturation into the Venetian society. The issue of interracial marriage could be seen as an attraction for Elizabethan audiences, and perhaps a controversial one. "It is obvious that Othello's tragedy would not have occurred in the same way it did if the Moor had not been of a different race and colour from most of those in the society about him. But the sense in which Othello's race and colour contributed to his downfall needs to be carefully distinguished from vague attributions of racial prejudice" (Salgado, 1985). Othello existed as a social lion in Venice, and undoubtedly felt racial isolation. "Notwithstanding the attention he received . . . Othello realized what the barrier of race meant, and was so modest as to hold an exaggerated sense of his personal deficiencies, "Rude am I in speech." When before the Senate it was only in his own opinion, "a round unvarnished tale" he could deliver, although in fact it was a perfect thing and charmed every ear. Later he laments the lack of attractions of conversation. . . ." (Givens, 1899). This lack of self-confidence and esteem is

---

2. Wild Man characters are non-European characters with varying levels of savagery.

typical of racial inferiority. Despite his accomplishments, Othello felt so inferior, that he was unable to fully measure his level of acculturation into the white society.

While Venice does not appear to be a racist society in the context of the play, the situation in Elizabethan England was one in which racial intolerance was starting to fester. "By the time Shakespeare's Othello appeared on the London stage in 1604, African characters of varying colours had become a familiar part of the London stage tradition. They were generally called Moors. Two broad types are distinguishable although they share some common characteristics" (Jones, 1965). The first type of Moor was noted for his extreme blackness and was villainous. The other type was of noble conduct and was seen as a "white Moor," a typical example being the Prince of Morocco in Shakespeare's *The Merchant of Venice* (Jones, 1965). "The presence of Negroes in England at about the same time is also clearly attested by Queen Elizabeth's edict in 1601 for the transportation of 'negars and blackmoores' out of the country, where their increased number was giving cause for alarm" (Jones, 1965). Against this background Shakespeare presented the Elizabethan audience with Othello. Indeed, Othello appears to incorporate the traits of both types of Moors. His role as noble soldier is well accepted by his peers, once he doesn't break the color barrier and become too intimate. "Brabantio's radically changed attitude when confronted with Othello as a son-in-law is revealing" (Salgado, 1985). Once he views Othello "as a professional soldier, Brabantio has nothing but admiration and affection for him. But forced to consider him in a more intimate relationship, he is trapped in the cultural stereotype of the black man as ugly, cruel, lustful and dangerous, near cousin to the devil himself" (Salgado, 1985). The Elizabethan audiences viewed this Moor as an exception to the rule—the exceptionally cultured Negro who has achieved some status. This view is reflected in the way Brabantio (as an image of his society) makes an exception and is prepared to accept Othello only as a soldier. In a similar way prejudiced people today make exceptions and admire black people for exceptional achievements in spite of their color (Salgado, 1985). Outside this arena, Othello is a stereotypical black man "and only witchcraft could account for a beautiful, intelligent and high-born maiden becoming enamored of him" (Salgado, 1985).

The play *Othello* does not really address the issue of racial integration and harmony (Salgado, 1985). The color difference between the married couple is not an impediment but a strength of their love. Desdemona even sees Othello as being invulnerable to the pangs of jealousy because of his birth—"I think the sun where he was born / drew all such humors from him" (III. iv). In spite of his strength, Iago is able to encourage Othello to see himself as an old black uncivilized Moor, which is at the root of any identity crisis Othello may entertain (Salgado, 1985). Low self-esteem is prevalent among blacks and other minorities during times of racial prejudice and suppression. "Thus Othello's colour is dramatically important as a symbol of his own uniqueness and the uniqueness of Desdemona's choice, but it is only when Othello begins to think of himself as a typical black man . . . that the seeds of tragedy are sown" (Salgado, 1985).

PURITY AND IMPURITY

Othello was written at a time when property ownership was a hot item in England. Approximately one-sixth of English land was changing hands by sale or lease, and the term 'surveyor' became prevalent in the English vocabulary around 1550 (Calderwood, 1989). The idea of property value has some parallel in *Othello*. To the Elizabethan audience Othello's blackness was a sign of impurity, while Desdemona's whiteness was a sign of purity. This is supported by the record of a performance of *Othello* in 1604 at Hallowmas (All Saints Day) festival in an English church. The two Shakespearean plays performed were *Othello* and *The Tempest*, and they were viewed as quite appropriate for that liturgical festival (Hassel, 1939). One comment on the two presentations was that "Hallowmas was a favorite time for testing the fidelity of lovers. *The Tempest* can refract that tradition romantically, and *Othello* tragically" (Hassel, 1939). The focus of the festival is the righteousness and persecution of saints and martyrs. *Othello* "bears the most attractive similarities to the festival. The day's theme of martyrs and persecuted blessedness is quickly suggested by Desdemona's suffering for her blessedness sake at the hands of an Othello who is himself ironically motivated by a strong, though perverted, sense of righteousness. Desdemona's whiteness of dress and skin, symbolizing her purity, even find their coincidental counterpart in the imagery of two prescribed readings from Revelation" (Hassel, 1939). Through the ritual of this religious festival, we see Desdemona as a saint who goes to her reward after death; and Othello as one who misjudged righteousness and must be punished for this crime (Hassel, 1939). Perhaps Othello's crime was being one of "them" and not one of "us"—of being black and not white. He is portrayed as damned through the Hallowmas ritual, and this damnation parallels the Eucharistic ritual of purity. "Ritual . . . is a major means of enclosing the pure and repelling the impure" (Calderwood, 1989). While the word 'Moor' had no real racial status in Elizabethan England, its first meaning in the Oxford English Dictionary suggested the reference to "infidel, non-christian, barbarian . . . at the lowest depths of depravity, a fellow Judas and the Prince of Darkness" (Calderwood, 1989). Calderwood further suggests that an element of possession existed in the Elizabethan attitude towards the whiteness of their skin, their language, history and social rituals when compared with those of the peoples of the New World. The Elizabethans commonly viewed the customs and people from the New World as dirty, and this was evident in the religious rituals. "Cleanliness then is not only next to godliness, it defines godliness. From this detergent standpoint Elizabethan England was godly indeed; having cleansed itself of a great deal of dirt, especially in the form of Catholics" (Calderwood, 1989). The dirty people were viewed as migrating to England to possess what the Elizabethans owned. Even the ones who didn't migrate were viewed as envious. These strangers were seen as the perpetual enemy—"an Arab, Jew, African, or Indian . . . was beyond salvation and beyond the law. If he were able and foolish enough to enter England he could not own property or bring any legal action. An infidel prudent enough to remain outside England but foolish enough to remain defenseless could be invaded, robbed and killed" (Calderwood, 1989). Of course these killings were viewed as an integral part of the Elizabethan's religious duties because infidels were part of the devil. The reference to Othello's 'sooty bosom' was a truth seen by Brabantio "who knew nature could not intend his daughter to mate with a black man, however noble" (Given, 1971). Othello is still an alien. No matter how noble his deeds, the blackness of his skin cannot be washed away. His presence on stage as an heroic black man in the midst of white Venetians, naturally sent a message to the

Elizabethan audience that a new type of Moor was in *their* midst. This is particularly poignant when we consider that the Elizabethan audience was aware of Queen Elizabeth's edict referred to earlier. The most noble reason for the edict according to the Queen's writings was that blacks are "infidels, having no understanding of Christ or his Gospel. The most obvious was that blacks are black, which means of course they are from the south. We all know what that means" (Calderwood, 1989).

In 1603 Sir John Davies exemplified this Elizabethan view of men from the south in his poem "Micrecosmos":

> . . . Southward, men are cruell, moody, madd,
> Hot, blacke, leane, leapers, lustfull, used to vant,
> Yet wise in action, sober, fearfull, sad,
> If good, most good, if bad exceeding bad.

But Othello is a black man who has been converted to Christianity and is viewed as having "crossed spiritual property lines" (Calderwood, 1989). He is on a journey to do what the Christians cannot do alone. Othello is a hired hand. He is in Venice on killing business. Obviously the "wealthy curled darlings of our nation" (*Othello* I. ii. 69) as Brabantio refers to his countrymen, cannot be expected "to bloody their doublets and muddy their hose fighting Turks" (Calderwood, 1989). Barbaric mercenaries like Othello are hired to do such work. There appears to be some parallel in the Venetians hiring Othello to kill Turks when Venice's property is threatened, and Othello's own murderousness when he believes that his own property, Desdemona, has been stolen. However, "the real surprise is finding the source of evil not in the devilish-looking black stranger, but in the honest-looking white citizen of Venice (Iago). Not the enemy outside like the Turks, or the stranger inside like the Moor, but the enemy who has always been inside . . . the enemy who is one of us" (Calderwood, 1989).

OTHELLO ELICITS SYMPATHY

In presenting Elizabethans with *Othello*, Shakespeare uses the presence of the Moor as tragic hero to confront the conscience of his countrymen. The play undoubtedly caused Elizabethans to reconsider their genetic place in the global structure, and their attitudes in the area of race relations. Shakespeare used the background of racial stereotypes and the social structure of Elizabethan England sensitively, "exploiting its potentialities for suggestion, but at the same time moving away from the stereotypes" (Jones, 1965). He presented the character of Othello in such a way as to compel sympathy from the Elizabethans (Given, 1899). In the end, the character of Othello emerges as a distinct individual and not a particular type of Moor. Hence his fall does not typify the weakness of Moors, but the weaknesses inherent in human nature (Jones, 1965).

REFERENCES

Calderwood, James L. (1989). *The Properties of Othello.* Amherst: The University of Massachusetts Press.

Given Esq., Welker. (1971). *A Further Study of the Othello— Have We Misunderstood Shakespeare's Moor?* New York: AMS Press. (quotes from the 1899 edition).

Greenblatt, Stephen J. (1990). *Learning to Curse—Essays in Early Modern Culture.* New York: Routledge.

Hassel Jr., Chris. (1939). *Renaissance Drama and the English Church Year.* Lincoln: University of Nebraska Press.

Jones, Eldred. (1965). *Othello's Countrymen—The African in English Renaissance Drama.* London: Oxford University Press.

Salgado, Ferella and Gamimi. (1985). *Shakespeare's Othello.* London: Penguin Books.

Wright, Louis B. and La Mar, Virginia A. (editors). (1967). Introduction to *Titus Andronicus*—"Popular Horror Plays," New York: Washington Square Press.

Wright, Louis B. and La Mar, Virginia A. (editors). (1956). Introduction to *Othello*—"The Significance of *Othello*," New York: Washington Square Press.

Anti-Semitism in Elizabethan Drama

Elmer Edgar Stoll

Elmer Edgar Stoll shows how the hatred of Jews that prevailed in Elizabethan society is mirrored in the plays of that time, most notably *The Merchant of Venice* and *The Jew of Malta*. The characters of Shylock and Barabas—from William Shakespeare and Christopher Marlowe's works, respectively—and Jews in other plays from the era are depicted as cruel, evil, and mercenary. Stoll argues that anti-Semitism was common in Elizabethan England, as well as much of Europe, so it is not surprising that these dramatists reflect such prejudice. Stoll was an influential critic of Shakespeare and other Elizabethan dramatists. His works include *Shakespeare and Other Masters* and *Shakespeare Studies: Historical and Comparative in Method*, a collection of essays he wrote during his career and the source of this article.

By all the devices . . . of William Shakespeare's dramaturgy Shylock [from *The Merchant of Venice*] is proclaimed, as by the triple repetition of a crier, to be the villain, though a comic villain or butt. Nor does the poet let pass any of the prejudices of that day which might heighten this impression. A miser, a money-lender, a Jew,—all three had from time immemorial been objects of popular detestation and ridicule, whether in life or on the stage. The union of them in one person is in Shakespeare's time the rule, both in plays and in 'character'-writing: to the popular imagination a money-lender was a sordid miser with a hooked nose. So it is in the acknowledged prototype of Shylock, Christopher Marlowe's 'bottle-nosed' monster, Barabas, the Jew of Malta [from the play of that name]. Though far more of a villain, he has the

Excerpted from *Shakespeare Studies: Historical and Comparative in Method*, by Elmer Edgar Stoll. Reprinted by permission of The Continuum Publishing Company.

same traits of craft and cruelty, the same unctuous friendliness hiding a thirst for a Christian's blood, the same thirst for blood outreaching his greed for gold, and the same spirit of unrelieved egoism which thrusts aside the claims of his family, his nation, or even his faith. If Barabas fawns like a spaniel when he pleases, grins when he bites, heaves up his shoulders when they call him dog, Shylock, for his part, 'still bears it with a patient shrug', and 'grows kind', seeking the Christian's 'love' in the hypocritical fashion of Barabas with the suitors and the friars. If Barabas ignores the interests of his brother Jews, poisons his daughter, 'counts religion but a childish toy', and, in various forms, avows the wish that 'so I live perish may all the world', Shylock has no word for the generous soul but 'fool' and 'simpleton', and cries ('fervid patriot' that he is, 'martyr and avenger'): 'A diamond gone, cost me two thousand ducats in Frankfort! The curse never fell upon our nation until now. I never felt it till now.' Such is his love of his race, which, Professor Walter Alexander Raleigh says, is 'deep as life'. And in the next breath he cries, as 'the affectionate father': 'Two thousand ducats in that, and other precious, precious jewels. I would my daughter were dead at my foot, and the jewels in her ear . . . and the ducats in her coffin.'

This alternation of daughter and ducats itself comes from Marlowe's play, as well as other ludicrous touches, such as your Jew's stinginess with food and horror of swine-eating, and the confounding of Jew and devil. This last is an old, wide-spread superstition: on the strength of holy writ the Fathers (with the suffrage in this century of Martin Luther) held that the Jews were devils and the synagogue the house of Satan. In both plays it affords the standing joke, in the *Merchant of Venice* nine times repeated. 'Let me say Amen betimes,' exclaims Salanio in the midst of his good wishes for Antonio; 'lest the devil cross my prayer, for here he comes in the likeness of a Jew.' And in keeping with these notions Shylock's synagogue is, as Luther piously calls it, *ein Teuffels Nest*, the nest for hatching his plot once he and Tubal and the others of his 'tribe' can get together. 'Go, go, Tubal,' he cries in the unction of his guile, 'and meet me at our synagogue; go, good Tubal, at our synagogue, Tubal!' In any one such eagerness for the sanctuary is suspicious; but all the more in those times, when the congregation was of Jews and the business of a Christian's flesh. These sly and insinuating

Oriental repetitions would of themselves have given the Saxon audience a shudder.

It is highly probable, moreover, that Shylock wore the red hair and beard, mentioned by Jordan, from the beginning, as well as the bottle-nose of Barabas. So Judas was made up from of old; and in their immemorial orange-tawny, high-crowned hats and 'Jewish gabardines,' the very looks of the two usurers provoked derision. In both plays the word Jew, itself a badge of opprobrium, is constantly in use instead of the proper name of the character and as a byword for cruelty and cunning.

THE DEPICTION OF JEWS IN ELIZABETHAN PLAYS

Now a popular dramatist, . . . even more than other artists, cannot play a lone hand, but must regard the established traditions of his art, the rooted sentiments and prejudices of his public. In other Elizabethan plays the Jew fares still worse. Few instances have come down to us; but in Abyssus in the anonymous *Timon,* Mammon in John Marston's *Jack Drum's Entertainment,* Pisaro in William Haughton's *Englishmen for My Money,* and Zariph in John Day's *Travels of Three English Gentlemen,* are to be found, in various combinations, usurer and miser, villain and butt, devourer of Christian blood and coin, and limb of the devil,—all big-nosed, or (in accordance with the vulgar error) foul of breath, in some fashion or other egregiously 'Jewy'. In Mammon and Zariph, who are manifestly done under the influence of Shylock, prominence is given to outcries of avarice and of gloating revenge; while in Pisaro and Abyssus it is the nose, enormous and fiery, that bears the brunt. All these figures, the monstrous births of feeble poets, which owe all the humanity they have to Barabas and Shylock, are nevertheless of the same class, and show the same traits, an exaggeration of the same comic spirit. If they are travesties, they are such unconsciously, inevitably.

In two other plays, which certainly antedate the *Merchant of Venice,* and probably the *Jew of Malta*—Robert Wilson's *Three Ladies of London* (1583) and the anonymous *Selimus* (1588)—the Jew has not developed so far. In the former play there is the single instance in the Elizabethan drama of an honourable Jew, one who forgives Mercatore a debt rather than let him go the length of abjuring his faith and turning Turk to escape it. But this episode is one with a purpose, that of satirizing the foreign merchants who are ruining England; and the Jews are painted fair only to blacken these. Gerontus is not held up to admiration as a whole, for his lending at interest is a practice bitterly attacked in this very play; but intent as he is on recovering only interest and principal, he serves admirably as a foil to a love of lucre that knows no bounds. That Wilson is no advocate of the race appears from his crediting to Usury, in his next play, *The Three Lords and Three Ladies of London,* a purely Jewish parentage. In the character of the usurer in Samuel Butler's and Thomas Overbury's collections, however, and in William Rowley's *Search for Money* (1607), the usual conception prevails—that of one who lends money at interest, hoards it, skimps both himself and his dependants, and is an egoist and an atheist without either virtue or conscience. Butler and Overbury do not call him a Jew, but Rowley is sufficiently explicit in giving him a nose like the 'Jew of Maltae's,' a foul odour, and Satan for patron. And the collections of medieval *exempla* abound in stories of usurers who are fonder of gold than of their own souls and have given them up for it to the devil. . . .

The closest parallel to Shylock and Barabas that I have seen is the Giudeo in Pretro Aretino's *Marescalco* (1526). He too is sly, fawning, and spiteful; and he even seems to have something of Shylock's trick of thought and speech.

In the Elizabethan drama and character-writing, then, the Jew is both money-lender and miser, a villain who hankers after the Christian's blood, a gross egoist, even an atheist (though charged with dealings with the devil), and at the same time a butt, a hook-nosed niggard. And a similar spirit of rude caricature and boisterous burlesque, with even less of characterization, prevails, we have seen, in the treatment of the Jew in early popular drama on the Continent. Such is the soil from which the figure of Shylock grew; for almost everything in Shakespeare is a growth, and strikes root deep in the present and in the past, in stage tradition and in the life about him.

ELIZABETHAN ATTITUDES TOWARD JEWS

The tradition having been examined, it now remains to examine the opinions, or antipathies, of the time,—a sorry tale to tell. Critics have wondered at the knowledge of Jewish character displayed by Shakespeare; but [nineteenth-century scholar] Sir Sidney Lee some years since showed that although banished from England in 1290, and not re-admitted until the latter days of Cromwell, Jews were then not unknown. 'Store of Jewes we have in England,' to quote *The Wandering Jew Telling Fortunes to Englishmen* (1640) [anon.]; 'a few in Court, many in the Citty, more in the Countrey.' In 1594, shortly before the *Merchant of Venice* was written, one of these Jews at court made something of a stir. Roderigo Lopez, the Queen's physician, was tried for conspiracy against her life. Sir Sidney Lee has shown the bitterness of feeling which it provoked, and the weight that was given to the fact that the offender was a Jew by prosecutor, judges, and people. 'The perjured and murderous Jewish doctor,' cried Edward Coke,[1] 'is worse than Judas himself'; and 'of a religious profession,' he said again, 'fit for any execrable undertaking.' Even his judges spoke of him as 'that vile Jew.' Though no longer a Jew by faith, when he protested from the scaffold that 'he loved the Queen as he loved Jesus Christ,' such words 'from a man of the Jewish profession,' says [sixteenth-century historian] William Camden, were 'heard not without laughter'; and 'He is a Jew!' men cried aloud as the breath passed from his body. 'And what's his reason?' asks Shylock in the play; 'I am a Jew!'

Of itself this incident is enough to show that although there was by no means a Jewish peril in Shakespeare's day, the race-hatred of Angevin times[2] had not burned out. Race-hatred, indeed, or the desire to profit by it, may have prompted the writing of this play, that Shakespeare's company might in the present excitement compete with Philip Henslowe's in their *Jew of Malta*. Even the Reformation, in England as in Germany, had done little to quench it: only the later Puritans felt any relentings towards the chosen race. . . .

Nor is it a legal or theological prejudice merely. Popular literature, like the drama, is, as we have already seen, imbued with it; and dozens of ballads, like *Hugh of Lincoln* and *Gernutus,* still handed it down orally from generation to generation. Enlightenment prevailed not against it. Many people think Shakespeare too free a spirit to have entertained it himself; but the freest spirit of Shakespeare's day, who, in a

---

1. Edward Coke was the Attorney-General of England during the Lopez trial. Coke later became Lord Chief Justice in 1613.   2. English rule under the Plantagenets, 1154 to 1485

short life, cast from him more hearsays and superstitions than any Englishman up to the time of [seventeenth-century philosopher] Thomas Hobbes, still clings to this. . . .

A SOCIAL HATRED

The frightful persecutions, the Jew-burnings, which at times of great emotional exaltation or depression raged through Europe in the thirteenth and fourteenth centuries, were almost always popular movements, not instigated or directed by the church; and princes, kings, emperors, popes like Clement VI, even fanatics like Saint Bernard, the Dominicans and the Franciscans, had, time and again, to interpose between the Jews and the violence of the mob. Converts fared little better than the faithful. And it was not the priest-ridden countries but those which first attained to a consciousness of national unity—England, France, Spain—as [nineteenth- and twentieth-century historian] Julius Wellhausen has shown, that expelled the Jews from their borders. In Italy, hard by the papal throne, they enjoyed greater security. In England, in the twentieth year of Henry III, the inhabitants of Southampton petitioned the king for a like privilege with the men of Newcastle, that no Jew should dwell amongst them, and Parliament granted Edward I a fifteenth in return for the favour of expelling the Jewish community as a whole. If, then, the hatred of Jews is at bottom a racial and social, rather than a religious, prejudice, and not Protestantism, not even the free thought of the Renaissance, but only Puritan fanaticism, late in the seventeenth century, availed, in any measure, to dispel it, why should we refuse to recognize it in Shakespeare, who, more than any other poet, reflected the settled prejudices and passions of his race?

History Plays United English Society

Germaine Greer

Germaine Greer assesses the role of historical playwrights during the Elizabethan era. She argues that the purpose of William Shakespeare's *Henry V* and other plays was to serve as propaganda that united the English people under the crown and raised morale. According to Greer, plays that portrayed Queen Elizabeth seditiously or fomented instability were censored and the playwrights possibly jailed. William Shakespeare, however, was usually successful in presenting an artificial version of English history that met with the approval of both the monarchy and the audience. Greer is a renowned feminist and literary critic. Her books include *Shakespeare*, the source of this essay.

The overriding concern of the historical dramatist was . . . to create an epic theatre, using all the resources of verse, music, and pageantry to project a vivid impression of the continuity of history and the audience's place in it. As William Shakespeare's fellow historian Samuel Daniel pointed out in his answer to Thomas Campion's[1] attack on rhyme, the historical poet's concern was at least partly mnemonic:

> All verse is but a frame of words confinde within certaine measure; differing from the ordinarie speache, and introduced, the better to expresse mens conceiptes, both for delight and memorie.

PROPAGANDA IN ART

The fame of the patriotic speeches in Shakespeare's histories is the best evidence that he succeeded in creating the incantations with which people stay their hearts in times of trou-

1. an English poet and composer who wrote a treatise on poetry

Reprinted from *Shakespeare*, by Germaine Greer (1986), by permission of Oxford University Press. Copyright © Germaine Greer 1986.

ble. The histories of the staging of Shakespeare could be supplemented by the story of the use of Shakespeare in wartime. In the darkest days of the siege of Malta (1941–3), to stir the hearts of the war-weary, groups of servicemen used to get up amateur radio performances of *Henry V.* Nowadays the art of 'psyching' people up for a superhuman effort has been elaborated into something rather sinister. By comparison Shakespeare's way of awakening dormant heroism in his audience is both modest and subtle.

For those people who believe that propaganda cannot be art, or that propaganda in support of causes of which they disapprove, such as loyalty to the monarchy, to a religious sect, or willingness to die for one's country, cannot be good art, the history plays will raise serious difficulties, which are only partly resolved if we decide to treat them as self-contained poetic entities or psychological studies of individual kings and nobles. For one thing, we will have to ignore a good deal of commentary presented by nameless characters, by representative characters, and by lay figures who appear for one important speech and are never seen again. For another, we will have difficulty with ghosts and portents, prophecies and curses, and we will have to ignore anachronistic contemporary references. *King John*, for example, contains various elements which have less to do with history than with propagandist intention—anti-papal (III. i), anti-Spanish (II. i. 23, 26; III. iii. 2, v. i. 65, v. ii. 151, 154, v. vii. 117), and pro-Elizabethan, in the parallels between John and Elizabeth—yet it is by no means crass or over-simplified. The complexity of the issues is never minimized, but thrown into dramatic relief by the selection of incidents and manipulation of sympathy. While we are drawn into the psychology and dynamic of conflict, at the same time dogmatism and faction are shown to be inappropriate responses, always involving more error than justification.

By the time he wrote *Henry V* (1598–9) Shakespeare must have been aware that the illusion of unity in English society could no longer be sustained. It was no longer in the power of the dramatist to hold the imagination of all, literate and illiterate, powerful and powerless. The development of the indoor theatres with their greater scenic resources and their prurient interest in matters sensational and intimate rather than public-spirited and universal had divided the Globe's audience while other entertainments vied for the groundlings' half-pence. The most talented newcomers to write for the theatre had a different viewpoint at once loftier and more limited.

A NEW VIEWPOINT

In 1598 a play of Ben Jonson's had been accepted for performance by the Lord Chamberlain's Men at the Curtain. Jonson had been imprisoned in 1597 for his part in the seditious play *The Isle of Dogs*,[2] the playing of which resulted in the closing of all the London theatres from July to October. Less than a year later he was tried at the Old Bailey for killing one of [theatrical entrepreneur] Philip Henslowe's players in a duel. He was convicted and escaped hanging only by pleading benefit of clergy. He was branded on the thumb and all his possessions confiscated by the Crown. He was practically unemployable in the theatre, but with the playing of *Every Man in His Humour* by Shakespeare's company his fortunes were reversed. It is therefore hardly to his credit that when he revised *Every Man in His Humour* he added a censorious prologue which could be thought to apply specifically to Shakespeare:

> Though need make many poets, and some such
> As art and nature have not better'd much;
> Yet ours for want hath not so loved the stage,
> As he dare serve the ill customs of the age,
> Or purchase your delight at such a rate,
> As, for it, he himself must justly hate:
> To make a child now swaddled to proceed
> Man, and then shoot up, in one beard and weed,
> Past threescore years; or, with three rusty swords,
> And help of some few foot and half-foot words,
> Fight over York and Lancaster's long jars,
> And in the tyring-house bring wounds to scars.

Jonson dismisses the whole epic theatre, together with the chorus that 'wafts you o'er the seas', the *deus ex machina*[3] descending from the clouds, depictions of hell-fiends surrounded by fireworks, and, significantly enough, tempests made by shaking shot in a sieve or playing drum-rolls. Jonson is concerned with 'realism' or 'truth to life', but Shakespeare deliberately eschewed this more insidious kind of illusion, knowing that the truest poetry was the most

---

2. Jonson co-wrote the play with Thomas Nashe. The text has since been lost.   3. in drama, a person or thing (originally a god in Greek and Roman plays) that appears out of nowhere and gives a contrived solution to a difficult situation

feigning. The apology he makes in *Henry V* is an inverted boast of his power to transport audiences to a vantage-point from which they could oversee and interpret their own history, and of their willingness to be so transported.

> And so our scene must to the battle fly;
> Where, O for pity! we shall much disgrace
> With four or five most vile and ragged foils,
> Right ill-dispos'd in brawl ridiculous,
> The name of Agincourt. Yet sit and see;
> Minding true things by what their mock'ries be.
>
> (IV, Chorus, 48–53)

THE DUTIES OF THE HISTORICAL DRAMATISTS

The historical dramatist had worse to fear than the sneers of the literati. No play would be licensed if it was thought to meddle in matters of politics or religion. . . . The deposition scene was removed from *Richard II* both on stage and in the printed quartos by about 1597, and the 1600 quarto of *Henry IV Part II* contained extensive revisions. A comparison of the 1594 quarto of *Henry VI Part II* with the version in the First Folio shows that all possible references to the Irish question,[4] Elizabeth's legitimacy, rebellion, or to particular noble families had at some stage been deleted from the text.

The licensing authorities could sniff out political and religious allegory in the most unlikely places. The old queen loved theatre; indeed she was herself a hieratic figure in an allegorical pageant of queenship which became more elaborate as she grew feebler. As she strained royal privilege to raise money for the war with Spain and parliamentary pressure for reform began to intensify, the common people were racked by a concatenation of visitations of plague, poor harvests, a wave of new enclosures, and economic recession. Fear of popular rebellion culminated in the law of 1595 prohibiting assemblies. The historical playwright had a clear brief; if he was not prepared to put together chronicles which would unite his audiences in their duty to God and the Crown, he had better stick to some other medium. In order to avoid the pitfalls of historical playwriting, it was not enough to refrain from trampling the Queen's corns. The playwright had to approach the struggle to subdue the tan-

---

4. In the 1590s, Ireland revolted against English efforts to incorporate it into the English administrative system. Although the Irish rebels did win some battles, England was ultimately victorious in 1603.

gle of confusing anecdote knowing what lesson he wanted it to teach and prepared to discard, distort, and invent in order to present his own version of the meaning of history. . . .

In an age when religious zeal turned brother against brother, the drama sought to reunite the people and raise public morale. Shakespeare was remarkably successful in managing potentially inflammable material so as to send audiences home excited and gratified rather than anxious about the deteriorating political situation and increasing instability of the Elizabethan order, but the plays are neither insipid or jingoistic. Shakespeare demonstrates his own version of the truism that those who fail to learn the lessons of history are compelled to repeat them; by signs, portents, and prophecies, events to come are foreshadowed while past causes are also tied in to present action, in each of the eight plays covering the two hundred years between the revolt of the Percys[5] and the accession of Henry VII. None is easy watching: not only must audiences follow attentively the fortunes of war expressed in emblematic skirmishes of a handful of soldiers with banners, drums and trumpets, and wooden swords, they must trace the endless permutations of subtle themes, constantly resurfacing in altered forms. The weaving together of the huge themes of right and wrong rule, of kingship as a divine office and a Machiavellian[6] political institution, of the reciprocal duties of ruler and ruled, against such a vast panorama is only possible in the theatre and then only in poetic drama.

5. The Percys were an English noble family, led by Henry Percy, Earl of Northumberland, his son Sir Henry Percy (also known as Hotspur) and the earl's brother Thomas Percy, Earl of Worcester. The Percys had been key supporters of Henry IV's accession to the English throne in 1399. However, by 1403 the family had revolted against the king. During that year, Hotspur died in a battle against the king and Thomas Percy was executed. The Earl of Northumberland formed another plot against the king in 1405 but was slain in battle at Bramham Moor in 1408.   6. Machiavellian is synonymous with amoral plotting. The term derives from Italian writer Niccolo Machiavelli, best known for his 1532 work *The Prince*, which describes how a prince can achieve and maintain power by being amoral and calculating.

CHAPTER 3

An Examination of William Shakespeare

Elizabethan Drama

Seneca's Influence on Shakespearean Tragedies

Brian Arkins

According to Brian Arkins, Roman dramatist Seneca was a major influence on the plays of William Shakespeare, particularly the tragedies *Titus Andronicus, Hamlet, and Macbeth,* and the history play *Richard III.* Shakespeare incorporates a number of features found in Senecan plays, including an obsession with crime, a ghost that desires revenge, and an emphasis on the supernatural. However, instead of merely copying Seneca, Shakespeare transforms many of his predecessor's conventions. Arkins is a professor of ancient classics at University College in Galway, Ireland.

'No author exercised a wider or deeper influence upon the Elizabethan mind or upon the Elizabethan form of tragedy than did Seneca.' So, rightly, T.S. Eliot. That influence is seen most obviously in Thomas Kyd's *The Spanish Tragedy* of 1586, in John Webster's *The Duchess of Malfy* of 1614 and in the plays of John Marston, but Seneca is also crucial to William Shakespeare, who may well have read his plays in Latin at Stratford grammar school. The revenge tragedies *Titus Andronicus* and *Hamlet* derive from Seneca, as do those plays of vaulting ambition *Richard III* and *Macbeth.* . . .

For the dramatists of the Renaissance in France, in Italy, and in England, Classical tragedy means the ten Latin plays of Seneca, not [Greek dramatists] Aeschylus, Sophocles, and Euripides; as [literary critics] Charles and Michelle Martindale say, 'Seneca was the closest Shakespeare ever got to Greek tragedy.' Indeed [literary critic] Francis Meres sees Shakespeare as a new Seneca: 'As Plautus and Seneca are accounted the best for Comedy and Tragedy among the Latins; so Shakespeare among the English is the most excellent in

Excerpted from "Heavy Seneca: His Influence on Shakespeare's Tragedies," by Brian Arkins, *Classics Ireland*, vol. 2 (1995). Reprinted by permission of the author.

both kinds for the stage.' No wonder, then, that Shakespeare himself, when he satirizes contemporary dramatists who mix the four recognized types of drama to the customer's taste, uses Seneca as a touchstone: 'Seneca cannot be too heavy nor Plautus too light' (*Hamlet* 2.2. 396–97).

For Seneca was in the Elizabethan air. Between 1551 and 1563 Cambridge was very Senecan, with two performances of *The Trojan Women*, two performances of *Medea*, and one of *Oedipus;* a landmark was clearly the staging of *The Trojan Women*, one of Seneca's best plays, in 1551. Then the first English tragedy *Gorboduc* [by Thomas Sackville and Thomas Norton], performed in 1562, was clearly Romanizing and was praised by Philip Sidney as 'climbing to the height of Seneca his style.' And, not least, the *Tenne Tragedies of Seneca* were translated into English by Jasper Heywood and others between 1559 and 1581, when they were published as a single book. These translations, which, as Eliot says, have 'considerable poetic charm and quite adequate accuracy, with occasional flashes of real beauty,' exercised a substantial influence on Elizabethan dramatists.

SENECAN FEATURES IN SHAKESPEARE

Shakespeare's most Senecan plays are *Titus Andronicus, Hamlet, Richard III*, and *Macbeth*, and the plays of Seneca that most contribute to these are *The Trojan Women, Phaedra, Thyestes, Agamemnon* and *Hercules Furens*. What Shakespeare derived from Seneca are the following seven general features, mediated, in part, through Italian Senecan plays such as the *Orbecche* of Giraldi Cinthio (1541):

1. An obsession with *scelus*, crime.
2. A preoccupation with torture, mutilation, incest and corpses—as in *Titus Andronicus.*
3. A stress on witchcraft and the supernatural—as in *Macbeth.*
4. The existence of vaulting ambition in the prince—as in *Richard III* and *Macbeth.*
5. The ghost that calls for revenge—as in *Hamlet* and *Macbeth.*
6. The self-dramatization of the hero, especially as he dies—as in *Hamlet* and *Macbeth.*
7. The frequent use of stichomythia[1] in dialogue, which

---

1. Stichomythia is dialogue, especially of altercation or dispute, which is delivered by two actors in alternating lines. It is a feature of classical Greek drama.

derives from passages like *Medea* 168—as in *Richard III* and *Hamlet.*

Seneca's influence is paramount in two of Shakespeare's revenge tragedies, *Titus Andronicus* and *Hamlet.* Widely regarded as Shakespeare's most Senecan play, *Titus Andronicus,* whose historical background is largely that of the fifth and sixth centuries AD, moves, like the plays of Seneca, 'towards a disaster for which the cause is established in the first minutes of action.'[2] First produced in the years 1590–92 and virtually absent from the London stage for centuries because of its horrors, *Titus Andronicus* invites us to contemplate multiple murders, human sacrifice, the cutting off of Titus' hand, the severed heads of Titus' sons, the rape, murder, and dismemberment of Lavinia, and a cannibal feast, in which Titus' mad cookery of Tamora's sons comes straight out of Seneca's *Thyestes;* as [twentieth-century critic] Kenneth Muir says, 'It is a nice irony that Shakespeare's most shocking play should be closest in spirit to the classics.'

Here Seneca is teaching Shakespeare how to make *scelus,* crime, a word that occurs more than 200 times in Seneca's plays, 'the central principle of tragic action and design, how to focus on the crime, the perpetrators, the victims, and on the moral framework violated.'[3] Indeed two of the most common tags from Seneca in Elizabethan drama deal with *scelus*: 'for crimes the safe way always leads through more crimes' (*Agamemnon* 115) and 'Great crimes you don't avenge, unless you outdo them,' which comes, significantly, from *Thyestes* (195–96). The word scelus, crime, occurs 38 times in Seneca's play *Thyestes,* which is an important influence on *Titus Andronicus.*

The revenge play, which is launched by *scelus,* comes in three phases, consisting of:

1. the appearance of the ghost or Fury;
2. the making of the revenger; and
3. the ritual revenge itself.

Shakespeare adapts this pattern in *Titus Andronicus* by sharing the revenge among three people, Tamora, who impersonates Revenge, Titus and Aaron. The most obvious representative of evil in the play—he is called by Waith 'an embodiment of evil'—the Moorish barbarian, Aaron, clearly

2. Eugene M. Waith, ed., *Titus Andronicus,* p. 69. Oxford, England: Oxford University Press, 1984.   3. Robert S. Miola, *Shakespeare and Classical Tragedy—The Influence of Seneca,* p. 16. Oxford, England: Clarendon Press, 1992.

recalls the hateful figure of Atreus in Seneca's *Thyestes*. But Titus, who, as a noble Roman father, contrasts with Aaron, turns into an avenger himself and serves up her children for Tamora to eat in a cannibal feast; 'Rome is but a wilderness of tigers' (3.1. 54). For, as we see from *Orbecche, Gordobuc*, and Thomas Hughes's *The Misfortunes of Arthur*, the spectacle of Kindermord [child murder] haunted the Renaissance.

For *Titus Andronicus* and for other plays, what Seneca offers Shakespeare, above all else, is an inimical universe in which evil triumphs—as the two direct quotations from Seneca's *Phaedra* attest. For Demetrius adapts *Phaedra* 1180 on the subject of Hell to articulate 'his consuming lust for Lavinia; his hell is emotional and psychological, a product of unruly passion,'[4] while Titus' outburst about the rapists' actions adapts *Phaedra* 671–72 to question God's tolerance of evil.

SENECA AND *HAMLET*

Discussion of Seneca's influence on *Hamlet* must begin with the remarks of [sixteenth-century English satirist] Thomas Nashe:

> Yet English Seneca read by candle light yeeldes manie good sentences, as Bloud is a beggar, and so foorth; and, if you intreate him faire in a frostie morning, he will affoord you whole Hamlets, I should say handfulls of tragicall speeches. But O griefe! tempus edax rerum, what's that will last alwaies? The sea exhaled by droppes will in continance be drie, and Seneca led bloud line by line and page by page at length must needes die to our stage.

It is not indeed that specific plays of Seneca's lie behind Hamlet, but that the whole tone of the play is Seneca; as [twentieth-century literary critic] Madeleine Doran puts it, 'Hamlet is certainly not much like any play of Seneca's one can name, but Seneca is undoubtedly one of the effective ingredients in the emotional charge of *Hamlet*. *Hamlet* without Seneca is inconceivable.'

Thematically, what Seneca gives to *Hamlet* is the general theme of revenge for a great wrong done; the ghost of Hamlet's father that seeks such a revenge and the extreme passion that characterizes Hamlet himself. Stylistically, what Seneca gives to *Hamlet* is the meditative soliloquy and stichomythia. There is therefore a general Senecan atmosphere in the play; as [twentieth-century critic] Robert Miola

4. Miola, p. 14.

says, 'The ghosts of Senecan drama—Atreus, Hercules, Pyrrhus, Clytemnestra, Aegisthus, Orestes, Electra[5]—and of neo-Senecan drama—Hieronimo, Titus, Lucianus[6]—hover in the background of *Hamlet*, providing perspective on character and action.'

Central to that perspective is the fact that Senecan conventions are often transformed in *Hamlet*. For example, Hamlet himself is not an avenger of the Senecan type who ruthlessly pursues his victim, but is something quite different, a man who, notoriously, wavers constantly before committing himself to revenge. Here Shakespeare exploits the Renaissance topos of an opposition between passionate action on the one hand and the Stoic ideal that passion in an infirmity on the other ('Give me that man that is not passion's slave'); at times, Hamlet sets out to be the Senecan avenger, at other times, he regards revenge with extreme misgivings. On the other hand, Claudius who displays lust, vengefulness, and greed for power is straight out of Seneca's *Aegisthus*.

The Senecan conventions are altered in other ways. While the ghost of Hamlet's father derives from the ghosts in Seneca's *Agamemnon* and *Thyestes*, unlike them, Hamlet's father modifies the call for revenge; 'nor let thy soul contrive / Against thy mother ought.' Again, Hamlet's famous meditative soliloquy 'To be or not to be' derives from a choral ode in Seneca's *The Trojan Women* lines 371–81.

Ambition in Shakespeare and Seneca

Two of Shakespeare's plays of vaulting ambition in the prince, *Richard III* and *Macbeth*, are also strongly influenced by Seneca. *Richard III* is called by Muir 'the most Senecan of Shakespeare's plays' and the play is clearly indebted to *Hercules Furens*, *Phaedra* and *The Trojan Women*. Richard himself is a typically Senecan tyrant, a gloomy, introspective, self-dramatizing hero, 'a spectacular character who dares scelus,'[8] he exemplifies extremely well the fact that evil is most potent when it lodges in the heart of the prince—as with Thyestes. Significantly, he revises that famous Senecan tag to 'But I am in / so far in blood that sin will pluck on sin' (4.2. 63–4).

5. Atreus is a character in *Thyestes*, Hercules is from *Hercules Furens*, Pyrrhus is a character in *The Trojan Women*, and the final four characters are from *Agamemnon*.   6. Hieronimo is from *The Spanish Tragedy*. Titus is the title character of *Titus Andronicus*. Lucianus is the character who represents Claudius in the play-within-the-play in *Hamlet*.   7. Stoics follow the tenets of the Greek philosophy of Stoicism.   8. Miola, p. 91.

One of the main Senecan features of *Richard III* is that Gloucester's[9] wooing of Anne derives from Lycus' wooing of Megera in *Hercules Furens;* as Hunter says, 'The whole Lycus/Megera situation in *Hercules Furens*—the usurping monarch seeking to strengthen his rule by forcing marriage on the wife of the vanished ruler—seems to be echoed in this scene.' To be specific: in both plays, there are similar preparations for entrance; appeals to general principles; the tyrant's wish for a softer answer, after a bitter one; his justification for past slaughter; and the violent reaction of the women who, clad in mourning, want the tyrant's death.

The climax of the wooing scene, the sword sequence, comes from Seneca's *Phaedra*. Just as the outraged Hippolytus holds a sword at the breast of the self-confessed criminal lover, Phaedra, who invites the stroke, so the outraged Anne holds a sword at the breast of the criminal lover, Gloucester, who invited the stroke. Faced with an eroticization of the situation, both Hippolytus and Anne drop the sword.

Finally, another important Senecan element in *Richard III* is found in the kommos[10] of Act 4, scene 4: the lamenting women, led by Margaret, who seeks to revile the tyrant, derive from the lamenting women in *The Trojan Women*, led by Hecuba.

MACBETH IS HIGHLY SENECAN

Macbeth, which was probably first performed at the Globe in 1606 and is one of the shortest of Shakespeare's plays, is 'a sophisticated recension of Senecan elements'[11] and so exemplifies what [nineteenth-century critic] William Hazlitt called 'the wildness of the imagination.' The Martindales usefully sum up Seneca's influence on *Macbeth:* 'There are a number of features in *Macbeth*—the heated rhetoric, the brooding sense of evil, the preoccupation with power, the obsessive introspection, the claustrophobic images of cosmic destruction—which recall Seneca's manner and interest, together with an unusually high number of passages which seem to derive from his plays.' Indeed the play constitutes Shakespeare's 'most profound and mature vision of evil'[12] and Macbeth himself is a criminal, an immoral man in

---

9. Richard, Duke of Gloucester; Richard's title before he is crowned King Richard III
10. Kommos is a musical exchange between character and chorus found in classical drama.   11. Miola, p. 93.   12. George Wilson Knight, *The Wheel of Fire: Interpretations of Shakespearean Tragedy*, p. 140. London: Methuen, 1965.

a moral universe, whose 'choice of evil unleashes catastrophic consequences which inflict the whole cosmos'[13]—a typically Senecan scenario. But *Macbeth* differs from *Richard III*: whereas Richard is the villain as hero, Macbeth is a hero who becomes a villain.'[14]

Detailed analysis of how Seneca's plays influence *Macbeth* must begin with Shakespeare's appropriation of two epigrams of Seneca that haunt the Elizabethan imagination; as Eliot says of Seneca, 'again and again the epigrammatic observation on life or death is put in the most telling way at the most telling moment.' At *Agamemnon* 115 Clytemnestra says *per scelera semper sceleribus tutum est iter,* which [sixteenth-century translator] John Studley translates as 'The softest path to mischiefe is by mischiefe open still'; this becomes Macbeth's 'Things bad begun make strong themselves by ill' (3.2. 55). At *Phaedra* 607 Phaedra says *curae leves loquuntur, ingentes stupent,* which Studley translates as 'Light cores have words at will, but great doe make us aghast"; this becomes Malcolm's 'the grief, that does not speak,/Whisters the o'er fraught heart, and bids it break' (4.3. 209–10).

But the Senecan play that most influences *Macbeth* is *Hercules Furens*, which Shakespeare must have re-read at this time. . . .

Macbeth's assertion (1.7.7) that 'We but teach / Bloody instructions, which being taught, return / To plague th' inventor' echoes Theseus' dictum in *Hercules Furens* that 'What each has done he suffers; the crime seeks out the author and the guilty one is crushed by his own form of guilt.' And, finally, Macbeth's reflection on Sleep in Act 2, scene 2, is based on the Chorus' reflections on Sleep in *Hercules Furens* 1065–81 (as well as in Ovid); with Macbeth's 'Sleep that knits up the revell'd sleeve of care, / The death of each day's life, sore labour's bath, / Balm of hurt minds, great Nature's second course, / Chief nourisher in Life's feast,' compare, in Heywood's translation 'And then O tamer best / O sleep of toyles, the quietnesse of mynde / of all the lyfe of man the better parte.'

In yet another debt to Seneca, Shakespeare makes Lady Macbeth find a paradigm for atrocious masculine daring in the character of Medea. Amid a framework of ritual incanta-

13. Charles and Michelle Martindale, *Shakespeare and the Uses of Antiquity: An Introductory Essay*, p. 38. London: Routledge, 1990.   14. Kenneth Muir, ed., *Macbeth.* London: Methuen, 1957.

tion, Lady Macbeth's countenancing of infanticide recalls Medea's murder of her children, and her command to the Spirits to 'unsex me here' recalls Medea's invocation to her own soul to 'Exile all foolish female feare and pity from thy Minde' (Studley). Finally, behind the secret, black and midnight hags who seek to bring about the damnation of Macbeth, lie the Furies of Greek mythology and of Seneca's *Thyestes*, terrible avenging sisters who are synonymous with witches and devils.

This astonishing catalogue of Senecan influence means that *Macbeth* rather than *Richard III* is 'the most Senecan of all Shakespeare's plays,'[15] and, since it is also one of Shakespeare's greatest plays, we can see that Seneca's influence was enormously beneficial.

15. Muir, *The Sources of Shakespeare's Plays*, p. 37. New Haven, CT: Yale University Press, 1977.

The Impact of Christopher Marlowe on the Works of Shakespeare

Muriel Bradbrook

William Shakespeare's most influential contemporary was Christopher Marlowe, writes Muriel Bradbrook. Marlowe's plays, particularly *The Jew of Malta*, helped shape the characterization of Shakespearean characters such as Shylock in *The Merchant of Venice* and Aaron in *Titus Andronicus*. According to Bradbrook, this influence was not one-sided, because Marlowe also reacted to the works of Shakespeare. Bradbrook was the first woman to hold a chair in the English Faculty at Cambridge University in England. She was an influential writer of theater studies whose works include *Themes and Conventions of Elizabethan Tragedy*.

'Who chooseth me shall gain what many men desire.'
Why, that's the lady! All the world desires her;
From the four corners of the earth they come
To kiss this shrine, this mortal-breathing saint.
The Hyrcanian deserts and the vasty wilds
Of wide Arabia are as throughfares now
For princes to come view fair Portia.
The watery Kingdom, whose ambitious head
Spits in the face of heaven, is no bar
To stop the foreign spirits, but they come
As o'er a brook to see fair Portia.
  (William Shakespeare's *The Merchant of Venice*, II, vii, 37–47)

At the moment of high ritual when the first of Portia's suitors, the Prince of Morocco, is to make his choice, a heightening of the verse attests his ardour. The dancing rhythm, with its onward flow, its panoramic view, and its refrain, is modelled

Excerpted from "Shakespeare's Recollections of Marlowe," by Muriel Bradbrook, in *Shakespeare's Styles: Essays in Honour of Kenneth Muir*, edited by Philip Edwards et al. Copyright © Cambridge University Press 1980. Reprinted with the permission of Cambridge University Press.

on Tamburlaine's speech at the death of Zenocrate.[1] Her apotheosis is celebrated with images of the cosmic grandeur that have marked Tamburlaine throughout, tinged here it would seem with some echoes of the Book of Revelations; Morocco uses the ritual of pilgrimage to express his reverence, although presumably his holy place is Mecca. . . .

THE JEW OF MALTA'S INFLUENCE ON SHAKESPEARE

Christopher Marlowe is found both at Belmont and Venice;[2] the main Marlovian connections, though more diffused, lie in Shylock's role.

In making use of *The Jew of Malta*, Shakespeare may have drawn on his own memories as an actor—for the play, unlike *Tamburlaine*, was not in print; but it had been put on by Lord Strange's Men in 1592, and was subsequently given by the Admiral's Men. If Edward Alleyn played Barabas, Richard Burbage as Shylock acquired a subtler version of the stage Jew.[3] Shakespeare took over certain situations, particularly from the role of Abigail the Jew's daughter, but Barabas's joy at the strategem by which his daughter recovers his gold from its hiding place—

> O my girl,
> My gold, my fortune, my felicity!
> . . .   .
> O girl! O gold! O beauty! O my bliss!—
> (*The Jew of Malta*, II, i, 46–53)

becomes Shylock's grief at the flight of Jessica as mocked by Solanio:

> I never heard a passion so confused,
> So strange, outrageous and so variable,
> As the dog Jew did utter in the streets.
> 'My daughter! O my ducats! O my daughter!' (II, viii, 12–15)

The subtle use of one Christian to entrap another was a practice of Barabas which Shylock greatly expands, when he pleads that the law of Venice, and international confidence in its stability, demand the fulfilment of his bond. That Antonio stands surety for Bassanio is not of Shylock's contrivance, as the mutual destruction of Mathias and Lodowick is of Barabas's.

Shakespeare can assume certain conventions about his

---

1. Tamburlaine is the title character of Christopher Marlowe's *Tamburlaine the Great, Parts 1 and 2*; Zenocrate is his wife.   2. the settings for *The Merchant of Venice*   3. Barabas is the title character in *The Jew of Malta*; Shylock is a character in *The Merchant of Venice*.

stage figure, and upon them work his own transformation. Barabas's justification for his treacheries, that 'Christians do the like', is sufficiently demonstrated; zest in planning these as a 'savage farce' had whetted the ironic plots in earlier plays, particularly *Titus Andronicus* and *Richard III,* where malignant delight in evil extrudes itself in lively action. The most direct borrowing from *The Jew of Malta,* Aaron's death speech in *Titus Andronicus,* is closely modelled on Barabas's counsel to Ithamore *(The Jew of Malta,* II, iii, 165–99),

> First be thou void of these affections:
> Compassion, love, vain hope, and heartless fear;   (ll. 165–6)

but becomes active;

> Even now I curse the day—and yet, I think,
> Few come within the compass of my curse—
> Wherein I did not some notorious ill.
>   *(Titus Andronicus,* v, i, 125–7)

The list of crimes that make up Barabas's life story include unprovoked murders (though of a secret kind) and more elaborate stratagems; beginning

> As for myself, I walk abroad a-nights,
> And kill sick people groaning under walls;
> Sometimes I go about and poison wells;
>   *(The Jew of Malta,* II, iii, 172–4)

and ending with the macabre image of a man hanging himself for grief, with pinned upon his breast a long great scroll 'how I with interest tormented him'. Aaron's crimes are more openly violent, but the list ends with an equally macabre image of death; he digs up dead men and sets them at

> their dear friends' door
> Even when their sorrows almost was forgot,
> And on their skins, as on the bark of trees,
> Have with my knife carvèd in Roman letters,
> 'Let not your sorrow die, though I am dead.'
>   *(Titus Andronicus,* v, i, 136–40)

The scrolls transform these two Death figures into emblems of Judgement, which lies beyond death.

As Aaron's last dying confession, an occasion when a man was expected to give an exemplary speech, and ensure his future life by dying well, his diabolic manifesto has more force than the counsel imparted to a slave, by reason of the position which it occupies. Unquenched evil holds its addict fast. Barabas's own death speech is comparatively short and entails a triumphant acknowledgement of what he has brought about, with a final curse on Christians and Turks alike. . . .

INFLUENCES ON EACH OTHER

Shakespeare's imitations of Marlowe, even at their closest, invite consideration of the differences between the two. Marlowe's was incomparably the most powerful dramatic voice which he encountered at the beginning of his career, and Tamburlaine's were the accents which first had liberated the drama. Blended with the voice of the Jew in Aaron is the voice of Tamburlaine, especially in his opening soliloquy:

> Now climbeth Tamora Olympus' top,
> Safe out of fortune's shot, and sits aloft,
> Secure of thunder's crack or lightning flash,
> Advanced above pale Envy's threatening reach.
>   . . .   .
> Away with slavish weeds and servile thoughts!
> I will be bright and shine in pearl and gold.
>
> (II, i, 1–4, 18–19)

The superb assurance of these lines, the triumph over Fortune, is Marlovian, in so grand a style that the fact that Aaron sacrifices his pride to secure the life of his bastard comes with a startling reversal. It is as if recalling Marlowe pushed Shakespeare into a further degree of inventiveness. This was the thesis maintained by [twentieth-century critic] Nicholas Brooke in the most cogent study of their relationship, 'Marlowe as Provocative Agent in Shakespeare's Early Plays'. As the sequence of history plays by Shakespeare and Marlowe ricochet one from another, each is seen borrowing in turn from the other. Henry VI's weakness shows the disintegrative force of a culpable innocence that lacks all will to power, and is in strongest contrast to Tamburlaine's power drive. Robert Greene's parody from that play in his warning, addressed to Marlowe, against Shakespeare,

> O tiger's heart wrapped in a woman's hide

is indeed the key to the catatonic movement by which Margaret [wife of King Henry VI] becomes a spirit of Nemesis. Finally, as the embodiment of evil, Richard Crookback [King Richard III] betters the Marlovian villain-heroes, for while they were pupils of Machiavelli[4] he could 'set the murderous Machiavel to school'. His opening speech also betters theirs, for he is his own prologue, whilst they are preceded by various kinds of chorus.

---

4. Italian writer Niccolò Machiavelli, best known for his 1532 work *The Prince*, which describes how a prince can achieve and maintain power by being amoral and calculating

Edward II, Marlowe's riposte, is clearly indebted to *Richard III*, since Mortimer's role as protector derives in some details from Richard's . . . but, as the study of an obsession, the play lacks that wider sense of the country's plight, the desolation of England's trampled garden, so prominent in Shakespeare's counter-play, *Richard II*. Here the plot of the deposed and libertine king has many parallels with Marlowe's, but whilst for instance the ritual of the deposition scene is greatly expanded, the homosexual element is so played down that Bushy, Bagot and Green seem almost irrelevant. Some of the Marlovian magniloquence heard in the opening scenes does not come from *Edward II*, but the earlier plays.

> I would allow him odds
> And meet him, were I tied to run afoot,
> Even to the frozen ridges of the Alps.   (*Richard II*, I, i, 62–4)

> O, who can hold a fire in his hand
> By thinking on the frosty Caucasus?   (I, iii, 294–5)

The two dramatists, contending with and reacting from each other, select their material to make contrasting effects. . . .

THE SONNET QUESTION

The question remains that this rivalry in the theatre may have accompanied rivalry outside the theatre. . . . Is Marlowe the rival poet of Sonnets 85 and 86?. . .

Sonnets 85 and 86, as I believe, describe a poetry contest between Shakespeare and the Rival Poet. These contests of recitation—one thinks of the *Mastersingers* of [German composer] Richard Wagner—had been held in London since Geoffrey Chaucer's time at the festival of the Pui (the guild of foreign merchants); at a lower level there were scolding matches or 'flytings'.

> Was it the proud full sail of his great verse,
> Bound for the prize of all-too-precious you,
> That did my ripe thoughts in my brain inhearse,
> Making their tomb the womb wherein they grew?
> Was it his spirit, by spirits taught to write
> Above a mortal pitch, that struck me dead?
> No.
>
> . . .   .
> But when your countenance filled up his line
> Then lacked I matter; that enfeebled mine.   (Sonnet 86)

Marlowe was so often credited with 'inspiration' by his fellow poets, with the 'brave translunary things' that made his spirits 'all air and fire' that the fifth line does not derogate from the recognisable fitness of the opening lines to Marlowe and to him alone. (George Chapman, chief alternative, had at this time written nothing, was only newly out of the Low Countries, and found composition extremely difficult and agonising by his own accounts.)

If Marlowe were the rival poet (and he seems to me the most likely candidate), this would explain why his verse reoccurred to Shakespeare in *The Merchant of Venice* within the high ritual atmosphere of a prize contest. In Sonnet 85 the winning poem was to 'reserve [its] character with golden quill', which was what happened to the prize poem at the festival of the Pui, where the winner was given a 'crown' for the song he had made in praise of the newly elected 'Prince' of that fraternity. It was then hung up under the 'Prince's'

MARLOWE'S DRAMATIC SKILLS

Frank Percy Wilson, a now-deceased lecturer at Trinity College, Cambridge University, in England, argues that Christopher Marlowe's dramatic skills have been underrated.

In any comparison between Marlowe and the early Shakespeare as dramatists there is a danger that Marlowe may suffer by reason of the degradation of his texts. He was . . . a man with a vocation for the drama, and no one could have met with his success who had not acquired a sufficient knowledge of stagecraft. It has been maintained that he is inferior to the early Shakespeare in 'the give and take of the dialogue, in which speeches are not merely juxtaposed but articulated', yet the most striking example in our early drama of one speech provoking and determining another is in 1 *Tamburlaine*, where Menaphon's parting line 'And ride in triumph through Persepolis' is caught up by the hero, and we watch it working and fermenting in his mind:

> And ride in triumph through Persepolis!
> Is it not brave to be a King, Techelles?
> Usumcasane and Theridamas,
> Is it not passing brave to be a King,
> And ride in triumph through Persepolis?

But the impression remains that in all that appertains to stagecraft and the technique of the theatre Shakespeare is superior.

F.P. Wilson, *Marlowe and the Early Shakespeare.* Oxford, England: Clarendon Press, 1953.

arms. (A mock challenge at wooing is set up in Ben Jonson's *Cynthia's Revels.)* In *The Merchant of Venice* the contest is for a much nobler reward; Morocco, the first contestant, departs with the mournful echo of what he had read on the scroll, 'Your suit is cold':

> Cold indeed and labour lost!
> Then farewell, heat, and welcome, frost,   (II, vii, 74–5)

whilst, after the interlude of Arragon (whom Nicholas Brooke compares with Marlowe's figure of the Guise in his contempt for things common), Bassanio approaches with that note of love and spring-time which is heard in the plays as well as the poems:

> A day in April never came so sweet
> To show how costly summer was at hand
> As this fore-spurrer comes before his lord.   (II, ix, 93–5)

The after-effects of [Marlowe's poem] *Hero and Leander* can be sensed in *Romeo and Juliet.* The resemblance is general and is a matter of the high assurance of Juliet's 'Gallop apace, you fiery-footed steeds', or Mercutio's bawdy wit (perhaps also the tragic suddenness of his death in a futile brawl may be taken to reflect Marlowe's own). The sustained note of lyric joy, the physical obstacles that separate the lovers, the blindness of destiny that opposes them do not add up to a challenge to Marlowe; they are in Shakespeare's own mode. . . .

SHAKESPEARE'S REACTIONS TO MARLOWE

Shakespeare's relation to Thomas Kyd, and to John Lyly, is often of a more detailed kind than his relation to Marlowe, for what they offered were theatrical models of rhetorical speech and dramatic patterning. What Shakespeare learnt from Marlowe, the only figure whose poetic powers approached his own, was shown rather in reaction. The greatest of Marlowe's creations, *The Tragical History of Doctor Faustus,* makes the least identifiable contribution; yet as Macbeth stands waiting for the sound of the bell, there is but one scene with which it may be compared.[5]

Psychologists affirm that the slighter the indication of an adjustment, the deeper its roots may well lie. Shakespeare reacted to Marlowe in a selective way, and as a person; that is to

---

5. At the end of *Faustus,* Faustus waits for the clock to strike twelve, signaling his death and descent into hell.

say, there is an emotional train of association in his borrowings. Marlowe, it is clear from *Edward II,* also reacted to Shakespeare; and Greene's warning to Marlowe may have gained in point and malice if the two were already known in some sense to be in contest for the poetic 'crown'. Such a contest, in the plague years, would have been part of the courting of favour that had survived in Spenser's day, but was by the mid 1590s not without its alternatives. To these Shakespeare returned, throwing in his lot with the common players.

Shakespeare's Comedic Style

Northrop Frye

Northrop Frye examines the comedic influences on William Shakespeare. Shakespeare is partly influenced by the Grecian dramatic styles of Old Comedy and New Comedy. This influence can be seen in Shakespeare's use of the themes of ritual resurrection and heroic triumph. However, Shakespeare transcends his influences, as his comedies ultimately reach a distinctive conclusion that cannot be associated with any previous style. Northrop Frye was an influential Canadian literary critic and professor whose works include *Northrop Frye on Shakespeare*.

The Greeks produced two kinds of comedy, Old Comedy,[1] represented by the eleven extant plays of Aristophanes, and New Comedy, of which the best known exponent is Menander. About two dozen New Comedies survive in the work of [Roman dramatists] Plautus and Terence. Old Comedy, however, was out of date before Aristophanes himself was dead; and today, when we speak of comedy, we normally think of something that derives from the Menandrine tradition.

THE PLOT OF NEW COMEDY

New Comedy unfolds from what may be described as a comic Oedipus[2] situation. Its main theme is the successful effort of a young man to outwit an opponent and possess the girl of his choice. The opponent is usually the father (*senex*), and the psychological descent of the heroine from the mother is also sometimes hinted at. The father frequently wants the same girl, and is cheated out of her by the son, the

1. Old Comedy was a dramatic style prevalent in the fifth century B.C.E. [Before Common Era]. It is highlighted by a chorus that sometimes takes part in the dialogue. The plot was resolved halfway into the play; long choral addresses and festivities marked the remainder of the play.   2. Oedipus was a mythological character who unknowingly killed his father and married his mother.

Excerpted from "The Argument of Comedy," by Northrop Frye, in *English Institute Essays*, edited by D.A. Robertson Jr., 1949. Reproduced with permission from the Columbia University Press, 562 W. 113th St., New York, NY 10025, via Copyright Clearance Center, Inc.

mother thus becoming the son's ally. The girl is usually a slave or courtesan, and the plot turns on a *cognitio* or discovery of birth which makes her marriageable. Thus it turns out that she is not under an insuperable taboo after all but is an accessible object of desire, so that the plot follows the regular wish-fulfillment pattern. Often the central Oedipus situation is thinly concealed by surrogates or doubles of the main characters, as when the heroine is discovered to be the hero's sister, and has to be married off to his best friend. In William Congreve's *Love for Love,* to take a modern instance well within the Menandrine tradition, there are two Oedipus themes in counterpoint: the hero cheats his father out of the heroine, and his best friend violates the wife of an impotent old man who is the heroine's guardian. Whether this analysis is sound or not, New Comedy is certainly concerned with the maneuvering of a young man toward a young woman, and marriage is the tonic chord on which it ends. The normal comic resolution is the surrender of the *senex* to the hero, never the reverse. William Shakespeare tried to reverse the pattern in *All's Well That Ends Well,* where the king of France forces Bertram to marry Helena, and the critics have not yet stopped making faces over it.

New Comedy has the blessing of Aristotle, who greatly preferred it to its predecessor, and it exhibits the general pattern of Aristotelian causation.[3] It has a material cause in the young man's sexual desire, and a formal cause in the social order represented by the *senex,* with which the hero comes to terms when he gratifies his desire. It has an efficient cause in the character who brings about the final situation. In classical times this character is a tricky slave; Renaissance dramatists often use some adaptation of the medieval "vice"; modern writers generally like to pretend that nature, or at least the natural course of events, is the efficient cause. The final cause is the audience, which is expected by its applause to take part in the comic resolution. All this takes place on a single order of existence. The action of New Comedy tends to become probable rather than fantastic, and it moves toward realism and away from myth and romance. . . .

In all good New Comedy there is a social as well as an individual theme which must be sought in the general atmos-

---

3. Causation is the agency that produces an effect. Aristotle lists four types of causes: material, formal, efficient, and final.

phere of reconciliation that makes the final marriage possible. As the hero gets closer to the heroine and opposition is overcome, all the right-thinking people come over to his side. Thus a new social unit is formed on the stage, and the moment that this social unit crystallizes is the moment of the comic resolution. In the last scene, when the dramatist usually tries to get all his characters on the stage at once, the audience witnesses the birth of a renewed sense of social integration. In comedy as in life the regular expression of this is a festival, whether a marriage, a dance, or a feast. Old Comedy has, besides a marriage, a *komos,* the processional dance from which comedy derives its name; and the masque,[4] which is a by-form of comedy, also ends in a dance. . . .

SHAKESPEARE'S COMIC INFLUENCES

It is only in Ben Jonson and the Restoration[5] writers that English comedy can be called a form of New Comedy. The earlier tradition established by George Peele and developed by John Lyly, Robert Greene, and the masque writers, which uses themes from romance and folklore and avoids the comedy of manners, is the one followed by Shakespeare. These themes are largely medieval in origin, and derive, not from the mysteries or the moralities or the interludes,[6] but from a fourth dramatic tradition. This is the drama of folk ritual, of the St. George play and the mummers' play, of the feast of the ass and the Boy Bishop,[7] and of all the dramatic activity that punctuated the Christian calendar with the rituals of an immemorial paganism. We may call this the drama of the green world, and its theme is . . . the triumph of life over the waste land, the death and revival of the year impersonated by figures still human, and once divine as well.

When Shakespeare began to study Plautus and Terence, his dramatic instinct, stimulated by his predecessors, divined that there was a profounder pattern in the argument of comedy than appears in either of them. At once—for the

4. Masques are short allegorical dramas performed by masked actors, popular in the sixteenth and seventeenth centuries.   5. the reestablishing of the English monarchy in 1660 under King Charles II   6. Mysteries, also known as miracle plays, present biblical stories or reenact saints' lives. Moralities are an offshoot of miracle plays that use allegories to teach Christian morals and ethics. Interludes are shorter plays, typically in dialogue, which developed from moralities but gradually involved more secular plots.   7. The St. George play presents the resurrection of St. George, symbolizing the rebirth of God. Mummers' plays are performed by masked actors and often in pantomime. The feast of the ass is a Christmastime play reenacting the flight of the holy family into Egypt. The Boy Bishop is a European custom during the Christmas season in which a boy was elected bishop, reigning until December 28 (Holy Innocents' Day).

process is beginning in *The Comedy of Errors*—he started groping toward that profounder pattern, the ritual of death and revival that also underlies Aristophanes, of which an exact equivalent lay ready to hand in the drama of the green world. This parallelism largely accounts for the resemblances to Greek ritual which [twentieth-century literary critic] Colin Still has pointed out in *The Tempest.*

The Two Gentlemen of Verona is an orthodox New Comedy except for one thing. The hero Valentine becomes captain of a band of outlaws in a forest, and all the other characters are gathered into this forest and become converted. Thus the action of the comedy begins in a world represented as a normal world, moves into the green world, goes into a metamorphosis there in which the comic resolution is achieved, and returns to the normal world. The forest in this play is the embryonic form of the fairy world of *A Midsummer Night's Dream*, the Forest of Arden in *As You Like It*, Windsor Forest in *The Merry Wives of Windsor*, and the pastoral world of the mythical sea-coasted Bohemia in *The Winter's Tale*. In all these comedies there is the same rhythmic movement from normal world to green world and back again. Nor is this second world confined to the forest comedies. In *The Merchant of Venice* the two worlds are a little harder to see, yet Venice is clearly not the same world as that of Portia's mysterious house in Belmont, where there are caskets teaching that gold and silver are corruptible goods, and from whence proceed the wonderful cosmological harmonies of the fifth act. In *The Tempest* the entire action takes place in the second world, and the same may be said of *Twelfth Night*, which, as its title implies, presents a carnival society, not so much a green world as an evergreen one. The second world is absent from the so-called problem comedies, which is one of the things that makes them problem comedies.

DEATH AND REVIVAL

The green world charges the comedies with a symbolism in which the comic resolution contains a suggestion of the old ritual pattern of the victory of summer over winter. This is explicit in *Love's Labor's Lost*. In this very masque-like play the comic contest takes the form of the medieval debate of winter and spring. In *The Merry Wives of Windsor* there is an elaborate ritual of the defeat of winter, known to folklorists as "carrying out Death," of which Falstaff is the victim; and

Falstaff must have felt that, after being thrown into the water, dressed up as a witch and beaten out of a house with curses, and finally supplied with a beast's head and singed with candles while he said "Divide me like a brib'd buck, each a haunch," he had done about all that could reasonably be asked of any fertility spirit.

The association of this symbolism with the death and revival of human beings is more elusive, but still perceptible. The fact that the heroine often brings about the comic resolution by disguising herself as a boy is familiar enough. In the Hero of *Much Ado About Nothing* and the Helena of *All's Well That Ends Well*, this theme of the withdrawal and return of the heroine comes as close to a death and revival as Elizabethan conventions will allow. The Thaisa of *Pericles* and the Fidele of *Cymbeline* are beginning to crack the conventions, and with the disappearance and revival of Hermione in *The Winter's Tale*, who actually returns once as a ghost in a dream, the original nature-myth of Demeter and Proserpine is openly established. The fact that the dying and reviving character is usually female strengthens the feeling that there is something maternal about the green world, in which the new order of the comic resolution is nourished and brought to birth. However, a similar theme which is very like the rejuvenation of the *senex* so frequent in Aristophanes occurs in the folklore motif of the healing of the impotent king on which *All's Well That Ends Well is* based, and this theme is probably involved in the symbolism of Prospero [from *The Tempest*].

The conception of a second world bursts the boundaries of Menandrine comedy, yet it is clear that the world of Puck [from *A Midsummer Night's Dream*] is no world of eternal forms or divine revelation. Shakespeare's comedy is not Aristotelian and realistic like Menander's, nor Platonic and dialectic like Aristophanes', nor Thomist and sacramental like Dante Alighieri's,[8] but a fourth kind. It is an Elizabethan kind, and is not confined either to Shakespeare or to the drama. Edmund Spenser's epic [*The Faerie Queene*] is a wonderful contrapuntal intermingling of two orders of existence, one the red and white world of English history, the other the

8. Platonic refers to the Greek philosopher Plato. In his philosophy, dialectics is the investigation of eternal ideas or forms. Thomist refers to St. Thomas Aquinas, a thirteenth-century theologian and philosopher. Dante's greatest work was *The Divine Comedy*, a poem that begins in tragedy (Hell) and ends in paradise (Heaven). It is considered a comedy because the story ends happily. Dante originally called the poem *Commedia* (Italian for comedy).

green world of the Faerie Queene. The latter is a world of crusading virtues proceeding from the Faerie Queene's court and designed to return to that court when the destiny of the other world is fulfilled. The fact that the Faerie Queene's knights are sent out during the twelve days of the Christmas festival suggests our next point.

COMEDY IN THE HISTORY PLAYS

Shakespeare too has his green world of comedy and his red and white world of history. The story of the latter is at one point interrupted by an invasion from the comic world, when Falstaff . . . throws his gigantic shadow over Prince Henry [in *Henry IV* Parts 1 and 2], assuming on one occasion the role of his father. Clearly, if the Prince is ever to conquer France he must reassert the moral norm. The moral norm is duly reasserted, but the rejection of Falstaff is not a comic resolution. In comedy the moral norm is not morality but deliverance, and we certainly do not feel delivered from Falstaff as we feel delivered from Shylock with his absurd and vicious bond. The moral norm does not carry with it the vision of a free society: Falstaff will always keep a bit of that in his tavern.

Falstaff is a mock king, a lord of misrule, and his tavern is a Saturnalia. Yet we are reminded of the original meaning of the Saturnalia, as a rite intended to recall the golden age of Saturn. Falstaff's world is not a golden world, but as long as we remember it we cannot forget that the world of *Henry V* is an iron one. We are reminded too of another traditional denizen of the green world, Robin Hood, the outlaw who manages to suggest a better kind of society than those who make him an outlaw can produce. The outlaws in *The Two Gentlemen of Verona* compare themselves, in spite of the Italian setting, to Robin Hood, and in *As You Like It* Charles the wrestler says of Duke Senior's followers: "There they live like the old Robin Hood of England: they say many young gentlemen flock to him every day, and fleet the time carelessly, as they did in the golden world."

In the histories, therefore, the comic Saturnalia is a temporary reversal of normal standards, comic "relief" as it is called, which subsides and allows the history to continue. In the comedies, the green world suggests an original golden age which the normal world has usurped and which makes us wonder if it is not the normal world that is the real Saturnalia. In *Cymbeline* the green world finally triumphs over a historical theme, the reason being perhaps that in that play the incarnation of Christ, which is contemporary with Cymbeline, takes place offstage, and accounts for the halcyon peace with which the play concludes. From then on in Shakespeare's plays, the green world has it all its own way, and both in *Cymbeline* and in *Henry VIII* there may be suggestions that Shakespeare, like Spenser, is moving toward a synthesis of the two worlds, a wedding of Prince Arthur and the Faerie Queene.

THE PHILOSOPHY OF SHAKESPEARE'S COMEDY

This world of fairies, dreams, disembodied souls, and pastoral lovers may not be a "real" world, but, if not, there is something equally illusory in the stumbling and blinded follies of the "normal" world, of Theseus' Athens with its idiotic marriage law, of Duke Frederick and his melancholy tyranny, of Leontes and his mad jealousy, of the Court Party with their plots and intrigues.[9] The famous speech of Prospero about the dream nature of reality applies equally to Milan and the enchanted island. We spend our lives partly in a waking world we call normal and partly in a dream world which we create out of our own desires. Shakespeare endows both worlds with equal imaginative power, brings them opposite one another, and makes each world seem unreal when seen by the light of the other. He uses freely both the heroic triumph of New Comedy and the ritual resurrection of its predecessor, but his distinctive comic resolution is different from either: it is a detachment of the spirit born of this reciprocal reflection of two illusory realities. We need not ask whether this brings us into a higher order of existence or not, for the question of existence is not relevant to poetry.

We have spoken of New Comedy as Aristotelian, Old Comedy as Platonic and Dante's *commedia* as Thomist, but it is difficult to suggest a philosophical spokesman for the form of Shakespeare's comedy. For Shakespeare, the subject matter of poetry is not life, or nature, or reality, or revelation, or anything else that the philosopher builds on, but poetry itself, a verbal universe. That is one reason why he is both the most elusive and the most substantial of poets.

---

9. Theseus is a character in *A Midsummer Night's Dream*; Duke Frederick is from *As You Like It*; Leontes is a character in *The Winter's Tale*; and the Court Party is from *The Tempest.*

Violence Toward Women in Shakespeare

Madelon Gholke Sprengnether

Madelon Gholke Sprengnether examines the ideas of
male dominance and violence (verbal and physical)
against women in William Shakespeare's plays.
According to Sprengnether, this violence is typically
directed toward women who are believed to be adul-
terous, such as Gertrude in *Hamlet* and Desdemona in
Othello. She explains that Othello, Hamlet, and other
male characters feel vulnerable, due to their belief
that women hold considerable power in their ability to
give and withhold love. Male dominance and violence
stems from this sense of vulnerability. Sprengnether is
the director of the English department at the University of Minnesota in Minneapolis. She is the co-editor
of *Shakespearean Tragedy and Gender.*

I shall, in the following pages, be considering the uses of
metaphor in several related ways. In some instances, I will
refer to the function of metaphor in individual discourse,
assuming that it is this kind of highly charged imagistic expression that offers the most immediate clues to unconscious awareness. I am assuming furthermore that metaphor may be seen to structure action, so that some features
of plot may be regarded as expanded metaphors. Moving
outward from this premise, I then want to consider the possibility that certain cultural fictions may be read metaphorically, that is, as expressions of unconsciously held cultural
beliefs. I am particularly interested in William Shakespeare's tragedies, in what seem to me to be shared fictions
on the part of the heroes about femininity and about their
own vulnerability in relation to women, fictions interweav-
ing women with violence, generating a particular kind of
heterosexual dilemma.

Excerpted from "'I Wooed Thee with My Sword': Shakespeare's Tragic Paradigms," by
Madelon Gholke Sprengnether, in *The Woman's Part: Feminist Criticism of Shakespeare*, edited by Carolyn Ruth Swift Lenz et al. Copyright ©1980 by Board of Trustees
of the University of Illinois. Used with permission from the University of Illinois Press.

METAPHOR IN ROMEO AND JULIET

The primacy of metaphor in the structures of individual consciousness, as in the collective fiction of the plot, appears in an early tragedy, *Romeo and Juliet,* where the failure of the play to achieve the generic status of comedy may be read as the result of the way in which heterosexual relations are imagined. In the conversation between the servants Sampson and Gregory, sexual intercourse, through a punning reference to the word "maidenhead," comes to be described as a kind of murder.

> *Sampson.* 'Tis all one. I will show myself a tyrant. When I have fought with the men, I will be civil with the maids—I will cut off their heads.
>
> *Gregory.* The heads of the maids?
>
> *Sampson.* Ay, the heads of the maids or their maidenheads. Take it in what sense thou wilt. (I. i. 23–28)

To participate in the masculine ethic of this play is to participate in the feud, which defines relations among men as intensely competitive, and relations with women as controlling and violent, so that women in Sampson's language "being the weaker vessels, are ever thrust to the wall" (I. i. 17–18). That Romeo initially rejects this ethic would seem to redefine the nature and structure of male/female relationships. What is striking about the relationship between Romeo and Juliet, however, is the extent to which it anticipates and ultimately incorporates violence.

Both lovers have a lively imagination of disaster. While Romeo ponders "some vile forfeit of untimely death" (I. iv. 111), Juliet speculates "If he is married, / My grave is like to be my wedding bed" (I. v. 136–37). Premonition, for both, has the force of self-fulfilling prophecy. While Romeo seeks danger by courting Juliet, and death by threatening suicide in the wake of Tybalt's death, Juliet, under pressure, exclaims: "I'll to my wedding bed; / And death, not Romeo, take my maidenhead!" (III. ii. 136–137). Read metaphorically, the plot validates the perception expressed variously in the play that love kills.

The paradigm offered by *Romeo and Juliet,* with some modifications, may be read in the major tragedies as well. Here, the structures of male dominance, involving various strategies of control, expressed in the language of prostitution, rape, and murder, conceal deeper structures of fear, in which women are perceived as powerful, and the heterosexual relation one which is either mutually violent or at least deeply threatening to the man.

MURDER IN THE BEDROOM: *HAMLET* AND *OTHELLO*

Hamlet's violent behavior in his mother's [Gertrude's] bedroom expresses some of the violence of his impulses toward her. Obsessed as he is with sexual betrayal, the problem of revenge for him is less a matter of killing Claudius than one of not killing his mother. Hamlet's anger against women, based on his perception of his mother's conduct, finds expression in the language of prostitution in his violent outburst against Ophelia: "I have heard of your paintings, well enough. God hath given you one face, and you make yourselves another. You jig and amble, and you lisp; you nickname God's creatures and make your wantonness your ignorance. Go to, I'll no more on't; it hath made me mad" (III. i. 143–48). It is painting which makes women two-faced, which allows them to deceive, to wear the mask of chastity, while lust "Will sate itself in a celestial bed / And prey on garbage" (I. v. 56–57). Like whores, all women cannot be trusted.

The paradox of prostitution in the tragedies is based on the masculine perception of the prostitute as not so much the victim as the agent of exploitation. If women are classed as prostitutes and treated as sexual objects, it is because they are deeply feared as sexually untrustworthy, as creatures whose intentions and desires are fundamentally unreadable. Thus, while Helen in *Troilus and Cressida* is verbally degraded, as the Trojans discuss her in terms of soiled goods and contaminated meat, she is, through her infidelity to Menelaus, the source of the sexual pride and humiliation that animate the entire conflict between the two warring nations. Honor among men in this play, though it takes the form of combat, is ultimately a sexual matter, depending largely on the fidelity or infidelity of women. For a man to be betrayed by a woman is to be humiliated or dishonored. To recover his honor he must destroy the man or woman who is responsible for his humiliation, for placing him in a position of vulnerability.

In *Hamlet,* it is the player queen who most clearly articulates the significance attributed to feminine betrayal. "A second time I kill my husband dead / When second husband kisses me in bed" (III. ii. 188–89). It hardly matters whether

Gertrude was implicated in the actual death of the elder Hamlet. Adultery is itself a form of violence and as great a crime. Hamlet, who reacts as an injured husband in seeking revenge against Claudius, also seeks retribution against his mother. Not having any sanction to kill his mother, however, he must remind himself to "speak daggers to her, but use none" (404). That his manner suggests physical violence is confirmed by Gertrude's response: "What wilt thou do? Thou wilt not murder me? / Help, ho!" (III. iv. 22–23). It is at this point that the violence that Hamlet seeks to contain in his attitude toward his mother is deflected onto another object presumed to be appropriate.

This single act of displaced violence, moreover, has further ramifications in terms of Hamlet's relation to Ophelia, whose conflicted responses to the killing of her father by her lover increase the burden of double messages she has already received from the men in the play and culminate in her madness and death. It is not his mother whom Hamlet kills (Claudius takes care of that) but Ophelia. Only when she is dead, moreover, is he clearly free to say that he loved her. Othello, in whom are more specifically and vividly portrayed the pathology of jealousy, the humiliation and rage that plague a man supposedly dishonored by the woman he loves, will say of Desdemona late in the play "I will kill thee, / And love thee after" (V. ii. 18–19).

THE FEMININE POSTURE

If I seem to be arguing that the tragedies are largely about the degeneration of heterosexual relationships, or marriages that fail, it is because I am reading the development from the comedies through the problem plays and the major tragedies in terms of an explosion of the sexual tensions that threaten without rupturing the surface of the earlier plays. Throughout, a woman's power is less social or political (though it may have social and political ramifications) than emotional, expressed in her capacity to give or to withhold love. In a figure like Isabella [in *Measure for Measure*] the capacity to withhold arouses lust and a will to power in someone like Angelo, whose enforcing tactics amount to rape. In Portia [in *The Merchant of Venice*], the threat of infidelity, however jokingly presented, is a weapon in her struggle with Antonio for Bassanio's allegiance. Male resistance, comic and exaggerated in Benedick [in *Much Ado About Nothing*], sullen and resentful in Bertram [in *All's Well That Ends Well*], stems from fears of occupying a position of weakness, taking in essence a "feminine" posture in relation to a powerful woman.

The feminine posture for a male character is that of the betrayed, and it is the man in this position who portrays women as whores. Since Iago occupies this position in relation to Othello, it makes sense that he seeks to destroy him, in the same way that Othello seeks to destroy the agent of his imagined betrayal, Desdemona. There is no reason to suppose, moreover, that Iago's consistently degraded view of women conceals any less hostile attitude in his actual relations with women. He, after all, like Othello, kills his wife. The difference between the two men lies not in their fear and mistrust of women but in the degree to which they are able to accept an emotional involvement. It is Othello, not Iago, who wears his heart on his sleeve, "for daws to peck at" (I. i. 62). Were it not for Othello's initial vulnerability to Desdemona he would not be susceptible to Iago's machinations. Having made himself vulnerable, moreover, he attaches an extraordinary significance to the relation. "And when I love thee not, / Chaos is come again" (III. iii. 91–92). "But there where I have garnered up my heart, / Where either I must live or bear no life, / The fountain from the which my current runs / Or else dries up" (IV. ii. 56–59).

Once Othello is convinced of Desdemona's infidelity (much like Claudio [in *Much Ado About Nothing*], on the flimsiest of evidence), he regards her, not as a woman who has committed a single transgression, but as a whore, one whose entire behavior may be explained in terms of lust. As such, he may humiliate her in public, offer her services to the Venetian ambassadors, pass judgment on her, and condemn her to death. Murder, in this light, is a desperate attempt to control. It is Desdemona's power to hurt which Othello seeks to eliminate by ending her life. While legal and social sanctions may be invoked against the prostitute, the seemingly virtuous woman suspected of adultery may be punished by death. In either case it is the fear or pain of victimization on the part of the man that leads to his victimization of women. It is those who perceive themselves to be powerless who may be incited to the acts of greatest violence.

The paradox of violence in *Othello*, not unlike that in *Macbeth*, is that the exercise of power turns against the hero. In this case the murder of a woman leads to self-murder, and the hero dies attesting to the erotic destructiveness at the heart of his relation with Desdemona. "I kissed thee ere I killed thee. No way but this, / Killing myself, to die upon a kiss" (V. ii. 357–58). If murder may be a loving act, love may be a murdering act, and consummation of such a love possible only through the death of both parties. . . .

MALE DOMINANCE AND FEMALE POWER

Violence against women as an aspect of the structure of male dominance in Shakespeare's plays may be seen to obscure deeper patterns of conflict in which women as lovers, and perhaps more important as mothers, are perceived as radically untrustworthy. In this structure of relation, it is women who are regarded as powerful and men who strive to avoid an awareness of their vulnerability in relation to women, a vulnerability in which they regard themselves as "feminine." It is in this sense that one may speak of a matriarchal substratum or subtext within the patriarchal text. The matriarchal substratum itself, however, is not feminist. What it does in Shakespeare's tragedies is provide a rationale for the manifest text of male dominance while constituting an avenue of continuity between these plays and the comedies in which women more obviously wield power.

Hamlet and Elizabethan Views Concerning Idleness

Paul A. Jorgensen

Paul A. Jorgensen explains that a great concern among Elizabethans, including William Shakespeare, was the shortness of life; Elizabethans felt guilty if they believed they were wasting time. The Shakespearean play that best exemplifies this belief is *Hamlet*, whose title character is slow to act in the wake of his father's murder by Hamlet's uncle and feels guilt over his idleness. According to Jorgensen, the theme of idleness found in the works of Shakespeare and his contemporaries is reflected in the views of Elizabethan theologians, who consider idleness a sin. Jorgensen is a professor of English at the University of California at Los Angeles. His books include *Shakespeare's Military World*.

Hamlet's displeasure with himself is mainly, but not entirely, derived from what he considers a failure to act. He does, however, act; hence the restlessness he displays is largely irrational. It is . . . wider in scope and significance than the plot which contains it. What Hamlet is expressing, and what William Shakespeare is expressing through Hamlet, is a restlessness, an urgency, an anxiety, more narrowly a time-consciousness, that is so general in the Renaissance that it may be loosely called the neurosis of the era. It is to be found in theological and philosophical treatises, in many of the major creative authors of the time, and in other plays of Shakespeare, principally those written within a period of about six years. I shall take up first Shakespeare's preoccupation with the theme of time-urgency, which is of course only a symptom of anxiety or restlessness.

Excerpted from "*Hamlet* and the Restless Renaissance," by Paul A. Jorgensen, in *Shakespearean Essays*, edited by Alwin Thaler and Norman Sanders. Copyright ©1964 by The University of Tennessee Press. Reprinted by permission of The University of Tennessee Press.

IDLENESS IN SHAKESPEARE

The sense of life's shortness haunted Elizabethans. Orlando's lines on the subject [in *As You Like It*] are more than
a pretty piece of versifying within an Arcadian setting; beneath them is an urgency that tormented most thoughtful
Elizabethans:

> Tongues I'll hang on every tree,
> That shall civil sayings show:
> Some, how brief the life of man
> Runs his erring pilgrimage,
> That the stretching of a span
> Buckles in his sum of age.

This urgency is effectively dramatized in a character created
some four years before Hamlet. Hotspur, although not in-
hibited in action, seems to feel the tyranny of time, the threat
of wasting it, almost as keenly as does Hamlet:

> O gentlemen, the time of life is short!
> To spend that shortness basely were too long
> If life did ride upon a dial's point,
> Still ending at the arrival of an hour.
>
> (1 *Henry IV*, V. ii. 82)

Prince Hal [later King Henry V] has only a somewhat less
poignant awareness of precious time. His seeming idleness
gives him occasionally a Hamlet-like sense of guilt:

> By heaven, Poins, I feel me much to blame
> So idly to profane the precious time. . . .
>
> (2 *Henry IV*, II. iv. 390)

In a play closer in time of composition to *Hamlet, Julius Caesar*, much of the tension of the early scenes derives from
Brutus' uncomfortable sense of a slowness to act. In *Troilus
and Cressida*, the idleness of Achilles (indeed the paralysis of
the entire Greek army) is given an intellectual, though not
highly dramatic, expression. Patroclus expresses the self-
reproach that grows within the heart of his friend:

> Omission to do what is necessary
> Seals a commission to a blank of danger,
> And danger like an ague subtly taints
> Even then when we sit idly in the sun.
>
> (III. iii. 230)

In all of these plays it may be argued that Shakespeare
was, with dramatic canniness, using time-anxiety to give
tension to the action, particularly to the flabbier parts; it is
noteworthy that the sense of haste is often conveyed at the
end of a scene. But this is to revert to [Shakespearean critic]

Elmer Edgar Stoll's kind of criticism, finding a dramaturgical expedient behind every psychological subtlety. Other Elizabethan writers, most of them nondramatic, express the same compulsion, the same sense of guilt in respect to the passing time. Of the major literary figures, we can here take up only three: Christopher Marlowe, Philip Sidney, and especially Edmund Spenser.

RESTLESSNESS AND ELIZABETHAN WRITERS

Marlowe's four major tragedies are of course dominated by restless spirits, men who find no peace unless they are stirring, and even then find no durable calm. Their painful, but exciting, creed is memorably expounded in the first of the plays, *Tamburlaine the Great:*

> Nature that fram'd us of foure Elements,
> Warring within our breasts for regiment,
> Doth teach us all to have aspyring minds:
> Our soules, whose faculties can comprehend
> The wondrous architecture of the world
> And measure every wandring plannets course,
> Still climing after knowledge infinite,
> And alwaies mooving as the restles Spheares,
> Wils us to weare our selves and never rest,
> Untill we reach the ripest fruit of all,
> That perfect blisse and sole felicitie,
> The sweet fruition of an earthly crowne.

All men are, in [twentieth-century literary critic] Harry Levin's phrase, overreachers; but behind the overreaching there is a restlessness seeking some relief in incessant action. John Bernard, writing on *The Tranquillitie of the Minde* in 1570, lists the four ways of life resorted to in an attempt to achieve quiet: those of the philosopher or learned man, the conquering prince, the wealthy or covetous man, and the voluptuous man. These correspond to the four restless ways of life dramatized in Marlowe's four tragedies. And of them all, Bernard says that they lead to no rest, but merely further striving. In Marlowe there is implied a need to use time to the utmost. What strikes one about this need, however, is its pointlessness. If Marlowe's restlessness has any philosophical basis, it is physiological or derived from the elemental agitation of the Lucretian theory.[1] No other great creative

---

1. Lucretius was a first century B.C.E. Roman poet and philosopher whose work focused on the ancient theory that everything, including the soul, is made of atoms. Thus, the soul is material and not immortal. Lucretius also thought that the laws of nature, not a deity, created the universe.

writer . . . is quite so unconscious in his sense of urgency. And no other writer is so totally lacking in a resolution to the restlessness.

Sir Philip Sidney displays in his *Arcadia* an occasional restlessness which ranges from an unexplained need for action to a tension derived from the demands of honor. Mainly it is the latter, though the pursuit of honor, as in Marlowe, can in itself be irrational. A typical passage is the following from the 1590 *Arcadia:*

> But as high honor is not onely gotten and born by paine, and daunger, but must be nurst by the like, or els vanisheth as soone as it appeares to the world: so the naturall hunger thereof (which was in Pyrocles) suffered him not to account a resting seate of that, which riseth, or falleth, but still to make one action beget another; whereby his doings might send his praise to others mouthes to rebound againe true contentment to his spirits.

This disinclination to find "a resting seate," this need "still to make one action beget another," is motivated not only by honor in Sidney but also by an ill-defined ambition, which confers an unwelcome sense of guilt upon any idleness. There is a Hamlet-like kind of self-recrimination in Sonnet XVIII from *Astrophel and Stella*, though, as with Milton's comparable sonnet, the sense of guilt may derive from the parable of the talents and hence be connected with the religious motivation which we shall later consider. Sidney writes:

> With what sharp checks I in myself am shent,
> When into Reason's audit I do go;
> And by just counts, myself a bankrout know
> Of all those goods which heaven to me hath lent.
> Unable quite, to pay even Nature's rent,
> Which unto it by birthright I do owe;
> And which is worse, no good excuse can show,
> But that my wealth I have most idly spent. . . .

Spenser's restless mood is almost unsurpassed. As with Marlowe there is an incessant need for achievement, and yet the conventional rewards of achievement are, as in Book II of *The Faerie Queene,* rejected as unworthy. But regardless of goal, what impresses one is that the knights are continuously restless in pursuit of some goal and that there are very few allowable moments for pause. The resolution achieved by victory is always a very brief one. Although Spenser's world sometimes suggests an inexplicable nightmare of striving, there is a fairly clear statement of man's necessary restless activity. It is a pursuit of an ethical ideal, usually subsumed under the name of honor, which makes inaction sinful. Thus Belphoebe speaks against the idle life of the court:

> Who so in pompe of proud estate (quoth she)
>   Does swim, and bathes himselfe in courtly blis,
>   Does waste his dayes in darke obscuritie,
>   And in oblivion ever buried is:
>   Where ease abounds, yt's eath to doe amis;
>   But who his limbs with labours, and his mind
>   Behaves with cares, cannot so easie mis.
>   Abroad in armes, at home in studious kind
> Who seekes with painfull toile, shall honor soonest find.

As in *Hamlet*, there are unallowable temptations to rest in *The Faerie Queene*. The mermaids of Book II offer Guyon entrance to the "Port of Rest" from "Paine and wearisome turmoyle"; but the Palmer sagely dissuades the youth from "that vanity" (II. xii. 32, 34). Suicide is proffered by Despair to the Redcrosse Knight as a means to "eternall rest" and its restful quality is expressed in one of the most beguiling stanzas of *The Faerie Queene* (I. ix. 40). But of course it is, as in *Hamlet*, merely a temptation to be overcome by the militant spirit in search of an ethical ideal.

Though *The Faerie Queene* is incomplete, and whatever solace finality of plot might contribute is denied us, Spenser does in places suggest an allowable rest. In the Mutability Cantos he seems to point, through religion, to

> that same time when no more Change shall be,
> But stedfast rest of all things, firmely stay'd
> Upon the pillours of Eternity.

But perhaps Spenser's, and the Renaissance's, noblest statement of allowable rest is that in the last stanza of "An Hymne of Heavenly Beautie":

> And looke at last up to that soveraine light,
> From whose pure beams al perfect beauty springs,
> That kindleth love on every godly spright,
> Even the love of God, which loathing brings
> Of this vile world, and these gay seeming things;
> With whose sweete pleasures being so possest,
> Thy straying thoughts henceforth for ever rest.

Admittedly this is not exactly the same kind of renunciation that Hamlet must make to achieve rest, but both Spenser and Shakespeare (at least in this one play) find no rest in what their heroes seek in the way of honor or revenge, and they turn to the stability and elevation of God. At any rate that is my reading of the resolution of *Hamlet*. Certainly, both Spenser and Shakespeare work toward a resolution, in a way that Marlowe does not.

THE THEOLOGICAL VIEW OF IDLENESS

From the theme of restlessness and time-tension in the major writers, I turn now to the more prosaic handling of that theme by . . . theologians. . . .

Divines and moral writers made idleness almost the greatest of sins. An official "Homily against Idleness" called it "a grievous sin." [Puritan author] Arthur Dent's extremely popular flagellatory treatise, *The Plaine Mans Path-way to Heaven* (1603), says of idleness that "it is the mother of all vices, and the stepdame of all vertue: yea, it is the great Beldame of all enormities." I could cite at least a dozen pious works admonishing against all kinds of inactivity. Some of these kinds seem merely quaint today. Sleep was grimly inveighed against, as in *Hamlet*. Even walking and gardening were causes of guilt feelings in certain individuals. One man, "beholding in this bysie age of the world, some imployed in the warres abroad, an honourable and now most needefull service, others in government at home, no lesse necessary," betook himself, as he told the Queen, to the one form of activity available to him: "bysied my selfe in turning my bookes to and fro." It is small wonder that Hamlet was concerned by his having forgone all custom of exercise.

Divines offered not only admonition but spiritual help for those afflicted by idleness. The assault upon "the filthie vice of slothfull idleness" is one of the principal spiritual battles for which there is a helpful prayer in Abraham Fleming's *A Monomachie of Motives in the Mind of Man* (1582). The titles of certain sermons indicate their stress upon making the most of man's limited and precious time: William Whately, *The Redemption of Time or A Sermon Contayning very good remedies for Those That Have Misspent Their Time* (1608); Roger Matthew, *The Flight of Time . . . Conducing to the Wise Numbering of Our Daies in the Sad Time of This Mortalitie* (1634); John Carpenter, *Time Complaining, Giveth a Most Godly Admonition* (1588). In this last work is made clear the theological reason for time anxiety. It was not merely that Satan finds work for idle hands. Rather it was the far more important fact that God gives us "his grace, to redeeme the time because the dayes are evill, to know the time of our visitation, and what belongeth to our peace, to seeke the Lord whiles he is near" (sig. A 6).

THE MEANING OF *HAMLET*

I hesitate to make the problem of salvation central to the meaning of *Hamlet,* though others have done so for Shakespeare's *Othello* and *King Lear.* Nevertheless, the audience could not have failed to regard any wasting of time as a grievous sin; and Hamlet himself, though he sometimes condemns his idleness in other terms, seems to have felt it as such. We must not be blinded by the revenge theme so that we overlook a deeper malaise. After all, we are not so distant from the Elizabethans but that we too are almost irrationally troubled by idleness.

CHAPTER 4

Assessing Elizabethan Drama

Elizabethan Drama

Elizabethan Drama Has Stood the Test of Time

Felix E. Schelling

Elizabethan drama has remained universally appealing, argues Felix E. Schelling. Although many of the plays are amateurish and flawed—in large part because the playwrights were given little time to complete their efforts—the literary value of Elizabethan drama as a whole has withstood the test of time. These plays remain interesting because they are universal, imaginative and focused on the events of their age. Schelling contends that modern drama lacks such qualities. Schelling was an educator and the author of various books of literary criticism, including *The Significance of Shakespeare* and *Elizabethan Drama, 1558–1642, Volume One*, the source of this article.

The English drama in the age of Elizabeth has been called above the most universal and imaginative, the most spontaneous and heterogeneous literature in dramatic form which has yet come from the hand of man. Its heterogeneity has already been sketched and will claim much attention in these volumes. As to these other qualities, Elizabethan drama may claim universality not only because much of it has a literary value to-day little tarnished by the lapse of ages but also because in its day it appealed to all classes, from the groundling, who stood on the cobbles under the open sky, to the plumed and brocaded knights and gentlemen who formed the most conspicuous and troublesome embellishment of the stage itself.[1] We know that a popular play was often raised and dignified by adaptation to a court performance. On the other hand, the queen herself occasionally condescended to witness a popular performance at the Blackfriars or the Globe, duly disguised and masked, as were all women

1. The most expensive seats in the Elizabethan theaters were onstage.

Excerpted from *Elizabethan Drama, 1558–1642*, by Felix E. Schelling (Boston: Houghton Mifflin, 1908).

of reputation who ventured within the public theaters of the day. In their zeal to preserve the peace and, as far as possible, the health of the city, the civic authorities of London opposed the theater. Their attacks were prompted by the antipathy which thrift always feels for extravagance, and encouraged by the growth of Puritanism, the austerity of which was hostile to the loose and thoughtless lives of many of those who acted plays or witnessed them. But as yet these attacks had assumed no very serious proportions and came from religious zealots like . . . John Field, satirists like Philip Stubbs, or renegade actors such as Stephen Gosson. Adverse criticism of the stage in the earlier years of Elizabeth's reign did not wean any considerable class of the London populace from its traditional pleasure in "shews;" and the drama still claimed the quality of universality in the continued strength of its appeal to the lower orders of society, as well as to those in whose children Puritanism was to beget a lively realization of the vanities of the world and a consequent partial withdrawal from them.

THE FUNCTION OF ELIZABETHAN DRAMA

It is easy to overlook the function which the Elizabethan stage actually performed in affording not only that amusement which belongs legitimately to the drama in all ages, but likewise that running comment on current affairs, that supply of news, of gossip, of sensational events, scandals, and crime, which is wont to be furnished us in modern times by our newspapers. In the height of the complexity of the Elizabethan drama the spirit that made men Englishmen responded to scenes representing the careers of adventurers . . . or to breezy dramas of action like Thomas Heywood's *The Fair Maid of the West* or *Fortune by Land and Sea;* or answered more vehemently to rude dramatizing of the repulse of the Spanish Armada, whilst a loftier genius moulded into artistic form the deeds of England's hero-king at Agincourt. The chronicle history flourished until an alien and un-English prince [King James I] succeeded to Elizabeth's throne and lost to the nation its sense of personal allegiance. In the hey-day of this great national utterance, the Elizabethan drama, no event was too trifling, no personage too august to be represented on the stage, if a matter of public interest. Dramatists, courtiers, and even ambassadors were satirized; the citizen was abused and lampooned, or absurdly glorified;

the faults, the whims, and the fashions of the day were represented and misrepresented. Plays had to be stayed and their writers imprisoned for matter of seditious or even of treasonable import. From 1598 for some years, a veritable "war of the theaters" raged, with varying fortunes in which Ben Jonson, armed with the artillery of the ancients, entered the lists against the long-bows, cross-bows, and blunderbusses of John Marston, Thomas Dekker and others. If we are to believe some interpretations of a celebrated passage in the satirical college play, *The Return from Parnassus,*[2] William Shakespeare himself was not without his part in these broils. Now all this is the full, bustling vigor of real life; agile, urgent, at times fatiguing, occasionally even disappointing; for the great Elizabethan age had its failures and half successes, its lapses from high ideals and its dullness too; but, none the less, full of hope and aspiration, full of the glory of youth and at times of the radiance of beauty, of the warmth, the glow, and the sincerity of truth.

Lastly, Elizabethan art was supremely imaginative; not introspective with that self-centered omnipresence of the ego which accounts for so much of the strength and the weakness of two such diverse poets as William Wordsworth and Lord Byron; nor yet analytic with that intellectualizing tendency which substitutes a mental process for an emotional delight and thus transforms art to the humble handmaiden of philosophy. Elizabethan literature, rightly read, has that rare quality, which may almost be called levity, of raising the reader above the point at which he merely understands, of disarming him of his critical panoply, and restoring to him once more that childlike openness of heart in which to understand is to enjoy.

THE SHORTCOMINGS OF ELIZABETHAN DRAMA

With these major qualities of universality, imaginativeness, and spontaneity once recognized, we may acknowledge the existence of minor shortcomings. Elizabethan drama as a whole is amateurish and unequal; at times it is scarcely literary. Outside of Jonson it is commonly wanting in design and effective elaboration; outside of Shakespeare its earlier efforts are unsustained and fragmentary; its later triumphs

2. *The Return from Parnassus* was an anonymous play performed by students at St. John's college in Cambridge in the early 1600s.

often studied or strained. Indeed, barring a few of the greatest, scarcely a play of the time is not open to criticism on the score of exaggeration, carelessness, improbability, or lack of finish. Nor could it well be otherwise, considering the conditions under which this drama was written. The demand was that of the moment, premeditation was usually impossible. At times a single play was let to two or three authors to be cobbled up in haste and learned by the actors before it was finished. Every acted play of the age was subject to incessant revision, excision, and recasting; and the laws of mine and thine commonly applied less to the authors than to the companies who were the real owners of the plays. With all this before our eyes and the purely temporary occa sion of the writing, we cannot but be lost in wonder that so many Elizabethan plays have stood the test of transportation across the centuries. Nor need this remain wholly unexplained. The drama of Shakespeare and his immediate fellows spoke to men by right of their manhood, not by virtue of their gentility. It stirred in its appeal the depths of a large and generous humanity. In the hands of John Fletcher and his successors the drama rapidly lost this universal character, and although continuing of high poetic and dramatic worth, began to appeal to a class, a dangerous restriction, in time to become a fatal taint. The drama began to lose, too, that firm foundation in ethics which alone can keep a literary production sweet for ages and tide it over to remain a living power to generations to come. The writings of Fletcher and of John Ford are of great literary excellence, but they mark the way step by step from the moral heights of the best Elizabethan plays to the moral depths of Restoration comedy, from the wholesome mirth of Shakespeare and his abiding faith in man to the soulless flippancy of William Congreve and John Vanbrugh, and the leering skepticism of William Wycherley.

Thus it was that in some eighty-five years[3] the English world was changed and with it the stage, its mirror. A history of the Victorian stage would present us with one phase of the multitudinous activity of that reign; a phase at its best scarcely literary, for the greatest plays of that age were either unacted or unactable; and the memorable dramatic names

---

3. the years spanning 1558–1642, beginning with the crowning of Queen Elizabeth I and ending with the outbreak of the English Civil War

of the times were not those of Percy Bysshe Shelley, Alfred Tennyson, Robert Browning, and Algernon Charles Swinburne, but Tom Taylor, Sheridan Knowles, and Bulwer, Lord Lytton. In Shakespeare's time the drama had not separated from literature and poetry; and although it might call in the aid of splendid scenic display, as did the masques, discuss a psychological problem or a problem of conduct, as does Shakespeare's *Hamlet* or Middleton's *A Fair Quarrel*, neither these things nor the claims of great actors could impair the splendid and imperishable literary form in which was conveyed a spirit inherently dramatic. Elizabethan drama is prëeminently interesting because it focused the activities of the age in itself and was literally a great national utterance. Modern drama is less interesting because it absorbs more of the individual and less of the time, because it habitually intellectualizes emotion and loses sight of the appeal of art in the zeal of the propagandist, in the curious minutiae of the psychologist or the perverted mania of the pornographist. In a word, modern drama is less interesting because it reflects a narrower range of ideas, and because, for the most part, it has discarded the sacred raiment of poetry.

Problems with Modern Productions of Elizabethan Drama

Alan C. Dessen

Alan C. Dessen suggests that modern directors should reconsider their approach to Elizabethan drama. According to Dessen, a return to the uncluttered stage of the Elizabethan theater would allow the audience to focus on the words and gestures of the actors without being distracted by excessive scenery and props. He also comments that directors should respect the multiplicity of plots in Elizabethan drama and not be so quick to reshape or edit the plays. Dessen is a Peter G. Phialas Professor of English at the University of North Carolina at Chapel Hill and the editor of the "Shakespeare Performed" section of the journal *Shakespeare Quarterly*. His books include *Elizabethan Drama and the Viewer's Eye*, from which this essay is excerpted.

No one actively engaged in a performance of a Shakespearean play need be reminded of the distinction between page and stage. In recent years, moreover, critics and scholars with considerable theatrical experience have been among the most active proponents of the "play on stage" point of view. Thus, in a provocative essay, John Russell Brown has taken to task any critic who pays lip service to "understanding the controlling importance of stage performance" but in practice uses "particular theatrical references, none too precisely, as a kind of exfoliation of his discourse on the play." Indeed, Brown sees the critical act as a distortion of the nature of drama, for attempts to "fix" plays—to "establish an inescapable revaluation"—represent a "wholly unwarranted simplification" of a medium which, in production, cannot be held still for examination. Brown's conclu-

Excerpted from *Elizabethan Drama and the Viewer's Eye*, by Alan C. Dessen. Copyright ©1977 by the University of North Carolina Press. Used by permission of the publisher.

sion, which he admits to be extreme, is that direct involvement, "at firsthand, with the process of a play in rehearsal
and performance is an inevitable step that must be taken by
the responsible critic of [William] Shakespeare's plays."

The strictures and arguments of Brown and others like
him, figures with credentials as critics, scholars, and directors, should carry a good deal of weight. Attempts to arrive
at a definitive explication of the meaning of any complex
play inevitably will be self-defeating, especially when the
critic does not take into account the many variables involved
in a production. Since critics and scholars often write for
each other, the director outside the academic community
has every reason to look with suspicion at yet another study
that purports to teach him his craft written by someone not
in the theater. Although theatrical insights often have flowed
into criticism and scholarship, the traffic in the other direction has been much lighter.

COMPARING MODERN AND ELIZABETHAN STAGING

Obviously, within a few pages I cannot convince a director
or actor of the utility of this study for his purposes. But let us
at least make a start with an interesting analogy. In 1941, a
major figure in the theater, Robert Edmund Jones, offered
the following evaluation of American drama in the 1930s.

> It is a truism of theatrical history that stage pictures become
> important only in periods of low dramatic vitality. Great dra-
> mas do not need to be illustrated or explained or embroi-
> dered. They need only to be brought to life on the stage. The
> reason we have had realistic stage "sets" for so long is that
> few of the dramas of our time have been vital enough to be
> able to dispense with them. That is the plain truth. Actually
> the best thing that could happen to our theatre at this mo-
> ment would be for playwrights and actors and directors to be
> handed a bare stage on which no scenery could be placed,
> and then told that they must write and act and direct for this
> stage. In no time we should have the most exciting theatre in
> the world.

Today we can recognize the truth in Jones's critique and appreciate some of the exciting events he prophesied. But there
is a revealing irony in his account. Here, in an age of stage
pictures and realistic sets, a highly knowledgeable figure
(whose credits include the designing of several major productions of Shakespeare's plays) cites the bare stage as an in-
novation, a step forward, a fruitful break with present prac-

tice. Though not specifically, Jones is arguing (consciously or unwittingly) for the advantages of Elizabethan over contemporary staging, since dramatists in the age of Shakespeare *did* have such a stage and *did* produce exciting theater. My purpose is not to belittle Jones (who may have had the Elizabethans in mind), but rather to note how modern dramatists and directors could be so immersed in the details of the present that they could lose sight of an instructive lesson from the past. A model was there, but few were looking.

Although it is relatively easy through hindsight to see both the assets and the liabilities in Jones's critique, to categorize what is "right" and "wrong" in our own theater is far more difficult. The most influential voice of recent years has been that of Antonin Artaud who argued for "no more masterpieces" and urged instead a theater of cruelty "in which violent physical images crush and hypnotize the sensibility of the spectator seized by the theater as by a whirlwind of higher forces." Peter Brook has commented upon Artaud's concept of a Holy Theater—"a theatre working like the plague, by intoxication, by infection, by analogy, by magic; a theatre in which the play, the event itself, stands in place of a text." Brook asks: "Is there another language, just as exacting for the author, as a language of words? Is there a language of actions, a language of sounds—a language of word-as-part-of movement, of word-as-lie, word-as-parody, of word-as-rubbish, of word-as-contradiction, of word-shock or word-cry? If we talk of the more-than-literal, if poetry means that which crams more and penetrates deeper—is this where it lies?" Brook's call for "another language" is linked to his sense of what is missing on the contemporary stage. He observes that "our ever-changing language has rarely been richer, and yet it does not seem that the word is the same tool for dramatists that it once was." Today, he argues, "writers seem unable to make ideas and images collide through words with Elizabethan force." One of the most successful modern directors of Shakespeare's plays is offering his critique of modern drama and using Elizabethan drama as one of his yardsticks.

But remember the critique (and the irony) supplied by Jones. If another sense of theater was available in Shakespeare's age but was not seen by the dramatists of the 1930s, is it not possible that "another language," especially "a language of actions," may also be there in Elizabethan plays al-

though largely unnoticed by later critics and directors? . . .
[Sixteenth-century English traveler] Fynes Moryson called
attention to the Elizabethan actors in Germany who somehow transcended the language barrier through their gestures and actions. If we have only recently discovered (or re-
discovered) the open stage, it may now be time to discover
(or rediscover) the techniques and visual language that go
with that open stage. The director who draws upon the skills
of the historian and the critic may be able to find "another
language" long lost but still recoverable, a language that
could add coherence and meaning to both Elizabethan and
later plays.

THE ADVANTAGES OF THE UNCLUTTERED STAGE

Such possibilities may seem grandiose, especially following
the rather modest claims based upon hypothetical stagings
of parts of Thomas Sackville and Thomas Norton's *Gorboduc,* George Wapull's *The Tide Tarrieth No Man,* and Shakespeare's *The Tempest.* But consider the added effect of dramatic emblems or visual analogues when acted out on a
bare stage (or hall or innyard)—with no scenery, with min-
imal use of props and accessories, with no attempt to sustain
any illusion of reality. As opposed to the extravagances of the
nineteenth century or the endless possibilities of the cinema,
such an uncluttered stage not only can free the audience's
attention for nuances of poetry but also can free the eye from
distraction so that it can focus upon the actors—their postures, their groupings, their costumes, and their part in a
patterned movement which is the entire play. In short, here
is a stage that can heighten both verbal and visual language.
Here moreover, is a stage upon which was played a body of
drama unequaled in our language with a dramaturgy that
has yet to be defined adequately and is not irrelevant to the
theater of today.

How then are we to define the dramaturgy or sense of theater that lies behind the plays we so much admire? Can we
even assume that one set of techniques or one idea of a theater can encompass the complex and diverse dramatic corpus of Elizabethan drama? For example, [literary critic]
Joseph W. Donohue, Jr., has pointed to the importance for
several centuries of English drama of "the affective drama of
situation"—an approach first associated with the plays of
John Fletcher who, at the end of Shakespeare's career, be-

came the most prominent playwright in London. In this kind of play, according to Donohue, "the intelligible unit is not the thematic part, placed within a coherent series of other parts, but, as in Fletcherian drama, the scene which exists in effect for its own sake." Such plays, whether Jacobean or Augustan or Romantic,[1] "have a structure based on a series of circumstances and events unconnected by a strict logic of causality (or Aristotelian 'action'); their situations are deliberately brought out of the blue for the purpose of displaying human reactions to extreme and unexpected occurrences."

In contrast to the plays of Fletcher and his successors, however, much of the preceding Elizabethan drama appears to be linked to a sense of "multiple unity" (a term advanced by Madeleine Doran and borrowed from art historians) in which many parts, rarely from only one story line, add up to a larger effect which draws upon a pleasure in "abundant variousness."[2] Extreme versions of such multiplicity of action (like Ben Jonson's *Bartholomew Fair*) become almost unintelligible on the modern stage, while, for pragmatic reasons, modern directors often will pare down the Elizabethan richness to fit a later sense of dramatic focus (the larger group of avenging sons—Fortinbras, Laertes, Pyrrhus—thus must give way to the story of Hamlet). Yet if we keep in mind the uncluttered stage and its potential for establishing visual relationships, we may find (as in my examples from *The Tide Tarrieth No Man* and *The Tempest*) interesting possibilities for a language of action or costume or gesture that could bring alive in the theater the linkages inherent in the concept of "multiple unity." To cite a familiar example, if we note that Brabantio in act 1 (with his mind poisoned by Iago) and Cassio in act 2 (with his degradation occasioned by giving in to his particular weakness) are acting out versions of Othello's tragic pattern, we may be able to stage the initial movement of the continuum that is *Othello* so that it visibly prefigures and illuminates the major sequence of the tragedy, even for an audience unaccustomed to such analogues.

---

1. Jacobean refers to the reign of King James I (1603–1625). The Augustan age is the name of an early eighteenth-century literary era. The term "Augustan" was used because the British writers used the themes and techniques of the poets who wrote during the original Augustan age—the reign of Roman emperor Augustus. The Romantic era was a literary movement of the late eighteenth and early nineteenth centuries.
2. Madeleine Doran, *Endeavors of Art: A Study of Form in Elizabethan Drama.* Madison: University of Wisconsin Press, 1954, p. 6 and *passim*.

LESSONS FOR THE MODERN DIRECTOR

The modern director can learn from the scholar or critic a different, perhaps a neo-Elizabethan, habit of mind, a way of seeing the personae and events of a Shakespearean play not only as an exposition of character but also as an unfolding of a larger pattern that can be enhanced and driven home by action, staging, and gesture. In such a pattern, units or sequences of plays have their own intrinsic interest yet can echo or prefigure each other, thereby yielding a complex multiple unity not apparent to the casual reader or to many an actor or director bound by his own sense of theater. Conversely, the excitement that a director gains by reshaping, cutting, or expanding an Elizabethan play may be at the expense of another kind of excitement present in the original that grows out of divergent parts coalescing into a larger whole before the eyes of the audience. By adding what he takes to be a comprehensible language for his viewers, that director may then be burying the original language which the playwright had incorporated into his own play.

At least part of the problem for directors and for many modern readers results from the complacent notions about "progress" that lurk (often unconsciously) beneath our attitudes toward the drama and culture of the past. It is difficult for anyone, including the historian, not to conceive of *The Tide Tarrieth No Man* and *The Cradle of Security*[3] . . . as "primitive," and such an evaluation often spills over into our attitude toward such accomplished dramatists as Christopher Marlowe, John Webster, and even Shakespeare. But we should remember that such plays apparently satisfied a diverse and demanding paying audience of the sort no longer drawn into the theater. Moreover, as Raymond Williams points out in his survey of modern drama, "the history of art is not one of continual evolution into higher and better forms; there is debasement as well as refinement, and a novelty, even a transformation, may be bad as well as good. It would be absurd to imagine that our own contemporary segment from the great arc of dramatic possibility is, because the latest, necessarily the best." Granted, there is no guarantee that attention to the distinctive nature of drama in the age of Shakespeare will yield results fruitful for the modern di-

---

3. *The Cradle of Security* was a morality play. Morality plays used allegories to teach Christian ethics.

rector. Yet we seem to be going through a lively period in the history of drama in which interesting steps forward or breakthroughs turn out to be (unwitting) rediscoveries of techniques taken for granted by Elizabethan audiences (the open stage, the mixing of actors and viewers, extempore improvisations based upon suggestions from the audience). The historian might prove an unforeseen ally for the innovative director.

The Continuing Influence of William Shakespeare

A.L. Rowse

According to A.L. Rowse, one of the great legacies of
the Elizabethan Age is its drama, most notably the
works of William Shakespeare. Rowse contends that
Shakespeare has had a significant influence on the
art and literature of the past four hundred years. In
addition, he contends, Shakespeare's plays helped
unite the modern English people. Shakespeare left
the greatest legacy of all the Elizabethan dramatists
because he best expresses the inner feelings and in-
stincts of the English. Rowse, who died in 1997, was
one of the twentieth century's great historians. His
work focused on the Elizabethan age and Shakespeare in particular. He wrote 90 books, including
Shakespeare the Man, Eminent Elizabethans, and *The
England of Elizabeth: The Structure of Society,* from
which this article is taken.

Vital in [England's] inheritance is the Elizabethan drama:
something unique, that is at the same time comparable to
the drama of Athens, which similarly expressed a great period of tension, of struggle and triumph in a small people's
history. Though we are used in our day to seeing plays of
Ben Jonson, Christopher Marlowe and John Webster—and,
especially in the universities, to occasional performances of
other dramatists of the time, Francis Beaumont and John
Fletcher, Thomas Dekker, Cyril Tourneur—the heart of the
matter is the prodigious vitality of William Shakespeare for
us. It may be seen in two aspects: the continuous and con-
tinually shaping influence of the work of Shakespeare on the
literature of his people and those who speak his language,
though not those alone. And there is the effect he has had,

Excerpted from *The England of Elizabeth: The Structure of Society,* by A.L. Rowse.
Copyright ©1950 by Macmillan Publishing Co., Inc. Copyright © renewed 1978 by A.L.
Rowse. Reprinted by permission of Macmillan Ltd.

and continues to have, on the minds of Englishmen. It is difficult to keep a sense of proportion about it, the phenomenon is so astonishing. No other literature has been so dominated by one writer as English literature has by him, not even Italian literature by Dante Alighieri, or Russian literature by Aleksandr Pushkin—perhaps the nearest parallels.

It is the phenomenon that is extraordinary, the illimitable vitality of his creations, the boundless influence of his work; for as a writer he was nothing if not natural. It was observed at the time that he was a child of nature, that he wrote as if by instinct rather than by following the rules; he was not an academic, bred in the universities, like Marlowe and Edmund Spenser, Robert Greene and George Chapman and Ben Jonson; least of all was he what would be called in our time an 'intellectual'—another name for the sterile and uncreative, the failed writer. Nor are his influence and inspiration confined to one country or the art of literature: one thinks of such works as Turgenev's *A Lear of the Steppes* or the plays of Victor Hugo, of Beethoven's *Coriolanus* overture, Verdi's *Otello* and *Falstaff,* Tchaikovsky's *Romeo and Juliet* and *Hamlet,* of Mendelsohn and Berlioz; or of . . . Elgar's *Falstaff,* and Vaughan Williams's *Sir John in Love* and *Serenade to Music.* The source of inspiration is apparently inexhaustible; even Soviet Russia . . . has contributed, with Shostakhovitch's opera *Lady Macbeth of Mzensk.* Or there are the provinces of the ballet and the film, just beginning to open up for him.

THE INFLUENCE OF SHAKESPEARE

But our concern is with his living part in our own tradition. In poetry one can trace his influence upon poet after poet, in some of them hear his accents—John Milton, John Dryden, Percy Bysshe Shelley, John Keats, Alfred Tennyson. (One thinks of Tennyson lying dead in the moonlight, with *Cymbeline* open beside him.) The historical novel springs—if after a long interval, so potent was the seed—from his imaginative treatment of history, his mingling of chronicle with characters of his own invention, come to fruition with the work of the most Shakespearean of writers, Walter Scott. Such characters as Hamlet, Falstaff, Lady Macbeth, Justice Shallow, Sir Toby Belch, Henry V,[1] inhabit the minds of mil-

---

1. from the following plays, respectively: *Hamlet, Henry IV, Parts 1 and 2* and *The Merry Wives of Windsor* (Falstaff), *Macbeth, The Merry Wives of Windsor, Twelfth Night* and *Henry V*

lions of those who speak their language: they are part of our mental world, none more potent or living, and help to bind us together, who are not severed by the seas. His essential concern with the problems of political and social order has only just begun to be recognised in literary criticism in the last few years. No other dramatist has devoted a whole cycle of plays to the history of the country, not only as a kind of dramatic epic, but as a morality, reflecting profoundly upon the problems of order and authority, the responsibility of kingship, the necessity of right governance in a community, of degree and difference of function, the punishment of guilty actions, retribution, the rough justice of time.

Or take the sphere of character, its values and tones, and our own tastes and predilections. There are, on the whole, two main types of women in Shakespeare: the spirited, quick-witted, independent Rosalinds, Beatrices, Portias, and the touching and tender Cordelias and Desdemonas[2] who are the innocent victims of fate. They have remained the dominant types of female character in the English novel. (In France it is the passionate, tempestuous woman, ultimately deriving from Jean Racine.) These Shakespearean types are really very English. It is sometimes asked, did he impose them by the power of his genius upon subsequent literature? Surely not: he must rather have expressed what was native to the English instinct, released preferences deeper and more subtle than of the mind, those of unconscious and natural choice.

In that lies the tremendous vitality and power of his work. There *is* something mysterious about Shakespeare to the English, as not a few of them have obscurely felt. It is nothing so crude as merely a concern with the facts of his life—about which we know as much as can be expected for the age; still less is it concerned with the harmless vagaries of the lunatic as to whether the townsman of Stratford could be the Shakespeare of the Plays, or whether he was not rather Francis Bacon or Queen Elizabeth, the Earl of Oxford or [the Earl of] Rutland or the Man in the Moon. The real mystery is the explanation of the inexhaustible vitality and veracity of all that he wrote, plays, characters, poetry or prose, for us English; so that centuries afterwards, in the stress of fighting for ex-

2. Rosalind is from *As You Like It*; Beatrice is from *Much Ado About Nothing*; and Portia is a character in *The Merchant of Venice*. Cordelia and Desdemona are from *King Lear* and *Othello*, respectively.

istence, in theatres disturbed by falling bombs and rockets, or in quiet English fields while the planes go over to Normandy, it is still his words that come to our lips. The mystery the English feel may be that this man of centuries ago should express them so completely today, should have expressed them, perhaps, for ever.

THE TWO HALVES OF THE ELIZABETHAN AGE

I think the explanation is to be found in the Age. The Elizabethan Age was so much the most intense and electric experience of a young people suddenly coming to maturity, with new worlds opening out before them, not only across the seas but in the mind. It is incredible what intensity of experience was crowded into those two decades at the end of Elizabeth's reign: one can only say here that the English

THE RISE OF ELIZABETHAN DRAMA

The drama of the late Elizabethan Age is considered to be one of the greatest achievements of that era. According to K.M. Warren, the artistry evident in the plays of William Shakespeare, Christopher Marlowe, and others is especially striking when compared to the lesser quality of the dramas of the mid-sixteenth century:

It is . . . in [Elizabethan] drama that we find all the well-known poets—with the exception of Edmund Spenser—putting forth their greatest force. The sudden rise of the drama in the latter half of the sixteenth century is the most remarkable phenomenon of this supremely remarkable literary age. It has never been fully accounted for. Many of the contemporary records concerning plays and the theatre have never been fully accounted for. Many of the contemporary records concerning plays and the theatre have undoubtedly been lost, so that we have to form our own judgment of Elizabethan dramatic literature and its causes upon, comparatively speaking, insufficient grounds. Out of some 2000 plays known to have been acted, only about 500 exist, as far as we know, and discoveries of new contemporary testimony or work might revolutionize our judgment on the history of Elizabethan drama. However that may be, the facts, as we have them, are that in the earlier half of the sixteenth century we find scarcely any dramatic work that would enable us to foresee the rise of the great romantic drama. Miracle-plays were acted up to 1579, but clearly no great development could come from these, and still less, people, in that short span, gave evidence of all that they had it in them to achieve in the centuries to come. All the myriad influences of Renaissance Europe, from Italy, France, the Low Countries, Spain and Germany, had come pouring in upon them, like so many waters finding their level: this island the last virgin soil to be fertilised. The islanders were a vigorous stock, with a history and a cultural tradition of their own, the most efficient State in Europe. They put up a long and obstinate resistance; they did not take at once to the charms of Renaissance culture and the inspiration of revived antiquity as the French did after Charles VIII's return from Italy. The new influences in thought and art worked slowly, leavening the English lump. How slowly may be seen from the fact that the Elizabethan Age itself falls into two halves. In the earlier, one sees a definite naïveté in both literature

perhaps, from the scholarly movement towards a so-called classical drama, imitations of the Latin comedies of Plautus and Terence, such as Nicholas Udall's "Ralph Roister Doister", named the "first English comedy", or the dramas of [Roman dramatist] Seneca, as in Thomas Sackville's and Thomas Norton's "Gorboduc", the "first English tragedy". There was also a popular tragi-comic drama of a somewhat rude kind (such as William Shakespeare travestied in the play of "Pyramus and Thisbe" in the "Midsummer Night's Dream"), but this was no more prophetic than the others. Then suddenly there appear between 1580 and 1590 plays with life, invention, and imagination in them, often faulty enough, but living. The predecessors of Shakespeare, George Peele, Robert Greene, Thomas Kyd, and others, but most of all that wild and poetic genius, Christopher Marlowe, "whose raptures were all air and fire", and who practically created our dramatic blank verse, prepare the way for Shakespeare. Rejecting, gradually, by a sort of instinct, those elements in the drama of the past that were alien to the English genius, they struck out, little by little, the now well-known type of Elizabethan romantic drama which in Shakespeare's hands was to attain its highest. And Shakespeare's genius made of it not only a vehicle for the expression of Elizabethan ideals of drama and of life, but a mouthpiece of humanity itself.

K.M. Warren, "English Literature," *Catholic Encyclopedia.* Copyright 1913, Encyclopedia Press, Inc. Transcribed by Douglas J. Potter, at http://www.knight.org/advent/cathen/05458a.htm. Electronic version copyright 1997, New Advent, Inc.

and art; the new influences are not yet assimilated; movement is like that of a young animal not yet sure of its mus-
cles or strength, learning to walk. There is a rawness and
rusticity, a gawkiness and stiffness even among Court poets
like Thomas Sackville or George Gascoigne, or in such productions as *Ralph Roister Doister* or *Gorboduc*, or *Gammer
Garton's Needle*.[3] It is like the stiffness and awkwardness in
the earlier wall-paintings and tapestries. But there is nothing
naïf about Shakespeare or Ben Jonson or John Donne, any
more than there is about Francis Bacon or [theologian]
Richard Hooker, [scientist and physician] William Gilbert or
[composer] John Dowland. *There* is a great difference between the earlier and the later half of the reign.

By the latter, all these influences from abroad and at
home, of Renaissance discoveries in the mind and the ex-
tension of actual experience in the world, of aesthetic and
intellectual excitement as well as scientific and geographical
exploration, of religious and philosophical questionings, had
all come together and fused themselves with the strong slow
English temperament, as in a crucible, with the testing time
of the struggle for life against Spain. It is noticeable how the
drama gets into its stride, and the madrigals begin, in those
very years of war, the fifteen-eighties. Such intensity of experience found fullest expression in Shakespeare. The most
absorptive and sensitive of instruments, he sensed all or
most of what there was in the time, releasing hidden depths
hitherto unexplored. He did not indeed express all that was
latent: religion, for example, had little or no appeal for him;
in that like the sceptical Michele de Montaigne. The truth
and fidelity of his recording lay in his very naturalness. He
trusted his instinct. If he had wanted to impose some intellectual construction of his own upon that upheaved world of
crowded experience his people were living through (what
an inspiration to a writer it must have been!), like Marlowe
or Spenser or Jonson or Donne, he would thereby have limited himself. By not doing so, he has escaped limitation; his
influence is therefore illimitable, is coterminous with the
life of the people he expressed and goes on continuously
with it. Therein lies the miracle. The release and *essor*
[scope] there is in his work he owed to the intensity of that

3. Nicholas Udall wrote *Ralph Roister Doister. Gorboduc* was written by Thomas
Sackville and Thomas Norton. The author of *Gammer Garton's Needle* is unknown.

moment in our history—as we owe to it the unfading memory of Elizabeth and him and Sir Francis Drake and all who made it theirs.

In the end, Shakespeare had no intellectual view of life, to the unity of which he subjugated the richness and variety of experience: in that, too, a mirror of his own people. His was not a metaphysical view of life; it was a moral and aesthetic one. Breaches of the moral order are brought home to the guilty; there is justice and retribution, even though the innocent suffer and there is much needless pain. There is a balance, a rough equilibrium in things. He is all for acceptance and conformity; after all, our souls are our own.

> Every subject's duty is the King's; but every subject's soul is his own.[4]

As for the stuff of life and experience we cannot lay hold of it; we cannot lay down rules for it; no religion completely contains or expresses or formulates it; at the heart of man is a dream.

> We are such stuff
> As dreams are made on, and our little life
> Is rounded with a sleep.[5]

Such are his words of farewell. The only possible expression of that attitude is poetry. And since in that, as in so much else, Shakespeare expresses the inner instinct of his people, it is natural that the poetic should be the characteristic medium of the English in the arts.

4. *Henry V*, IV. i. 189.   5. *The Tempest*, IV. i. 156.

Shakespeare's Importance Has Been Overstated

Gary Taylor

The greatness of William Shakespeare has been over-stated by literary scholars, argues Gary Taylor. Shake-speareian critics are too often sycophantic, unwilling to approach the plays and poems as being anything other than the works of a genius. According to Taylor, Shakespeare was a talented writer but not one who should be treated as especially unique. Taylor is the director of the Hudson Strode Program in Renaissance Studies at the University of Alabama at Tuscaloosa. He has written and edited numerous books, including the complete works of Shakespeare and Thomas Middle-ton. Taylor is also the author of Reinventing Shake-speare: A Cultural History, from the Restoration to the Present, the source of the following essay.

William Shakespeare cannot claim any unique command of theatrical resources, longevity or reach of reputation, depth or range of style, universality or comprehensiveness. But critics continue to exalt him. . . .

By overestimating Shakespeare's importance and unique-ness, Shakespearian critics insult the truth. They glorify one writer by denigrating many.

EDITING CONUNDRUMS

But they also harm Shakespeare himself. For instance, if we believe that Shakespeare's work was perfect and all-encompassing, we cannot edit it. If everything he did was done ideally, then anything in the extant texts that dips tem-porarily beneath our own waterline of perfection will be stigmatized as corrupt, textually corrupt, a blemish of trans-mission that should accordingly be emended out of exis-

Excerpted from *Reinventing Shakespeare*, by Gary Taylor. Copyright ©1989 by Gary Taylor. Reprinted by permission of Artellus Ltd., London.

tence, so that the text can float back up to the surface of our (and its) complacency. In such circumstances, editing becomes unending cosmetic surgery, the face perpetually reshaped to suit the latest fashion. Alternatively, if we believe that Shakespeare's mind was all-encompassing, singular by virtue of its unique plurality, not limited by the artificial boundaries of a physical mind or a local time, then the extant texts can hardly be emended at all. Even the most contorted phraseology, for which his own work and the work of his contemporaries offer no parallels, and which might easily arise from the simplest and commonest of printing errors, even such readings just might be another instance of Shakespeare's limitless and therefore wholly unpredictable genius—a genius so all-swallowing that those who have dared to fault him have been filleted by subsequent scholarship for the paucity of their own understanding. For such editors it is unsafe to emend anything, because Shakespeare is so much smarter than you that your cleverness today will inevitably look like stupidity tomorrow. It is safer to praise than to think.

In pondering whether or not to emend, editors have to decide what Shakespeare actually did or did not write. Such problems extend beyond the authority of individual words to the authenticity of whole works. The Victorian and Edwardian campaign that [literary critic and scholar] E.K. Chambers epitomized and stigmatized as "The Disintegration of Shakespeare" depended in part upon the belief that England's perfect poet could do no wrong; therefore, if something in his plays, or even whole plays, seemed bad, the offending bit must have been writ by some lesser wit. (Such attitudes have not disappeared; in the controversy over the authenticity of "Shall I die?" we were repeatedly assured that Shakespeare could not have written such a "bad" poem.) Hermeneutics accomplishes the same act of critical salvation with a similar formula: if Shakespeare wrote something that appears to be awful, then in fact it must be brilliant, if only you look at it carefully enough. Blemishes need not be emended, if all blemishes can be redefined as beauty marks.

Such editorial and critical maneuvers attempt to cope with apparent defect in a canon arbitrarily predefined as fault-free, Shakesperfect. Another strategy extends the physical boundaries of a canon already arbitrarily predefined as unboundable. Critics sometimes claim, for instance, that it doesn't really matter whether or not Shakespeare wrote all of *All Is True*.[1] In one sense, this is true; the work should be judged independently of its origin. But this socialist theory (that works of art are not private property, that authorship doesn't matter) leads in practice to a monopolistic corporate takeover (as Shakespeare appropriates the entire work). Since Shakespeare's "comprehensive soul" could have written anything, one might as well assume that it did write everything. As Lewis Theobald expressed the prejudice in 1728, "my Partiality for *Shakespeare* makes me wish, that Every Thing which is good, or pleasing, in our Tongue, had been owing to his Pen."

SHAKESPEARE'S LIMITATIONS

This attitude is still operating. In 1968 two critics independently related aspects of *Timon of Athens* to the comedies of Thomas Middleton. Brian Gibbons, in an influential book on *Jacobean City Comedy*, suggested that "Shakespeare in Act III of *Timon of Athens* may be indebted to Middleton's art of comedy." Philip Edwards observed that if *Timon* had not survived, "we should not have known . . . of Shakespeare's power to write satirical merchant comedy in a style which only Middleton could equal." Neither scholar records the fact that doubts about Shakespeare's authorship of the whole of *Timon of Athens* had been regularly expressed since 1840 and that Middleton had been independently nominated as his collaborator by two investigators in the early 1920s. Since 1968, studies by David Lake, MacDonald P. Jackson, R.V. Holdsworth and myself have shown that, on the evidence of every independent objective linguistic criterion, Middleton, not Shakespeare, wrote Act Three of *Timon of Athens,* the scenes that demonstrate such a remarkable gift for "satirical merchant comedy." The proposed proof of Shakespeare's unpredictable range emerges in retrospect as a demonstration of his predictable limitations; Shakespeare could not write urban satire of Middleton's caliber, Middleton's caustic comic intelligence. But Philip Edwards continues to attribute *Timon* wholly to Shakespeare, ignoring recent scholarship as confidently as he ignored earlier scholarship. In the same way, critics and theatres continue to credit Shakespeare with the whole of *Macbeth* and *Pericles*

---

1. an earlier title for *Henry VIII*

and *All Is True,* despite the relentless accumulation of evidence that parts of each were written by others. The same aggrandizing impulse has led scholars at one time or other, for some reason or other, to attribute to him every competent play—and some incompetent ones—written in the 1580s or early 1590s. Thus in 1986, Eric Sams gave Shakespeare sole credit for every play included in the First Folio, as well as the anonymous plays *Edmund Ironside, Edward III, The Troublesome Reign of King John, The True Chronicle History of King Leir, The Famous Victories of Henry V,* and a lost early play on Hamlet, among others.

Moreover, if Shakespeare was perfect, then he never needed to revise any of his work. This attitude was articulated by his first editor, Nicholas Rowe, discussing Shakespeare's habits of composition:

> Perhaps we are not to look for [*Shakespear's*] Beginnings, like those of other Authors, among their least perfect Writings; Art had so little, and Nature so large a Share in what he did, that, for ought I know, the Performances of his Youth, as they were the most vigorous, and had the most fire and strength of Imagination in 'em, were the best . . . what he thought, was commonly so Great, so justly and rightly Conceiv'd in it self, that it wanted little or no Correction, and was immediately approv'd by an impartial Judgement at the first sight.

This statement—which, with the rest of Rowe's "Account of the Life," was prefixed to every major edition for a century—sets the problem of revision within the prevailing critical dichotomy between Nature and Art. Since Shakespeare did not pay any attention to the "rules" of dramatic writing, as they were understood by the eighteenth century, then he could not owe the success of his plays to any "Art," any critical artifice, at all; he depended upon "Nature," which naturally expressed itself in his first thoughts. Within the system of critical discourse available to Rowe, Shakespeare could be defended only as an exemplar of Nature; Nature did not revise; therefore, Shakespeare did not revise.

This attitude has long outlived the critical vocabulary that gave it birth, despite the steady accumulation of textual and historical witnesses against it. When confronted by two early versions, both purportedly by Shakespeare, editors since Rowe and Pope have simply asserted that one text or the other is corrupt. Indeed, by the end of the eighteenth century the antipathy to revision had actually hardened. Rowe and Pope were willing to admit that Shakespeare made mistakes; a century later, such fault-finding had come to seem disrespectful. Once Shakespeare was enthroned as an infallible genius, it became almost impossible to believe that he revised his work. God doesn't make mistakes, and God doesn't change his mind. Editing and criticism since the eighteenth century have defined "Shakespeare" in a way that makes it logically impossible for "Shakespeare" ever to have revised his own work; their definition, as [philosopher] Ludwig Wittgenstein would say, "fills the whole of logical space, leaving no point of it for reality."

SHAKESPEARE IS A BLACK HOLE

A singularity (represented by the symbol *) is the center of a black hole; it is a mathematical point in space having no length, breadth or depth, a point at the center of a once vast, now collapsing star where matter is crushed by its own irresistible gravity into literally zero volume. Even light cannot escape from a black hole; time itself stops.

If Shakespeare has a singularity, it is because he has become a black hole. Light, insight, intelligence, matter—all pour ceaselessly into him, as critics are drawn into the densening vortex of his reputation; they add their own weight to his increasing mass. The light from other stars—other poets, other dramatists—is wrenched and bent as it passes by him on its way to us. He warps cultural space-time; he distorts our view of the universe around him. As Ralph Waldo Emerson said, "Now, literature, philosophy, and thought are Shakespearized. His mind is the horizon beyond which at present we do not see."

But Shakespeare himself no longer transmits visible light; his stellar energies have been trapped within the gravity well of his own reputation. We find in Shakespeare only what we bring to him or what others have left behind; he gives us back our own values. And it is no use pretending that some uniquely clever, honest, and disciplined critic can find a technique, an angle, that will enable us to lead a mass escape from this trap. If Shakespeare is a literary black hole, then nothing that I, or anyone else, can say will make any difference. His accreting disk will go on spinning, sucking, growing.

Before he became a black hole, Shakespeare was a star—but never the only one in our galaxy. He was unusually but not uniquely talented. He was indeed singular, not because he surpassed all other writers, but simply because he was a unique and unrepeatable individual, living in a unique and unrepeatable time and place. He was no less and no more singular than anyone else. Shakespeare remains, like every other somebody, like us but not us. We are attracted and defeated, educated and mystified, by his strangeness, his otherness, his contradictory incompleteness, his whole, his holes, his permanent personal opacity, his multiplicity. He reinvented himself imaginatively and prolifically, but not infinitely. He, too, was limited, confined by space and time and the boundaries of his own perception. He is not us. But he is like us. The culture that turns him into a god produces a schizophrenic criticism, mixing abasement and appropriation.

Within our culture, Shakespeare is enormously powerful. Power corrupts and disfigures. The power of a politician easily corrupts his entourage, and the power of a poet easily corrupts his apologists. The courtier/critic's "candied tongue," in Hamlet's withering description, will all too readily "licke absurde pompe, / And crooke the pregnant hindges of the knee." But criticism, at its best, struggles to be free; like the press at its best, its function is to doubt what we have been told; it is skeptical; it is suspicious of power. Sycophancy is no more admirable in literature than in politics.

CHRONOLOGY

1532

Niccolò Machiavelli writes *The Prince*

1533

Elizabeth, daughter of King Henry VIII of England and Anne Boleyn, born

1542

Mary Queen of Scots, daughter of King James V of Scotland and Mary of Guise, born

1547

King Henry VIII dies, succeeded by son King Edward VI

1553

King Edward VI dies, succeeded by half-sister Queen Mary I

1558

Queen Mary I of England dies, succeeded by half-sister Queen Elizabeth I

1561

Francis Bacon born

1564

William Shakespeare born; Christopher Marlowe born

1565

Thomas Sackville and Thomas Norton write *Gorboduc*

1566

James, son of Mary Queen of Scots and Lord Darnley, born; Nicholas Udall writes *Ralph Roister Doister*

1567

Mary Queen of Scots forced to abdicate, succeeded by son James who becomes King James VI of Scotland

1572

Ben Jonson born

1576

The Theatre built in London

1577

Publication of Raphael Holinshed's *Chronicles*; the Curtain and Blackfriars theaters open in London

1577–1580

Sir Francis Drake circumnavigates the globe

1584

Sir Walter Raleigh founds first English colony in Virginia

c. 1586

Thomas Kyd writes *The Spanish Tragedy*

1587

Mary Queen of Scots executed; Thomas Hughes writes *The Misfortunes of Arthur*

c. 1587–1588

Marlowe writes *Tamburlaine the Great, Parts I and II*

1588

English navy defeats Spanish Armada

c. 1588

Marlowe writes *The Tragical History of Doctor Faustus*

1589

Marlowe writes *The Jew of Malta*

1590

First three books of Edmund Spenser's *The Faerie Queene* published; Philip Sidney's *Arcadia* published

1591

Shakespeare writes *1 Henry VI*

1591–1592

Shakespeare writes *2 Henry VI* and *3 Henry VI*

1592

The Rose theater opens

c. 1592

Marlowe writes *Edward II*

1592–1593

Shakespeare writes sonnets, *The Comedy of Errors,* and *Richard III*

1593

Marlowe dies in a tavern fight; Shakespeare writes *Titus Andronicus, The Taming of the Shrew, The Two Gentlemen of Verona, Love's Labour's Lost* and the poem *Venus and Adonis*

1593–1594

Plague in London shuts down theaters

1594

Lord Chamberlain's Men formed; Shakespeare's poem *The Rape of Lucrece* published; Robert Greene writes *Friar Bacon and Friar Bungay*

1594–1595

Shakespeare writes *A Midsummer Night's Dream, Romeo and Juliet,* and *Richard II*

1595–1596

Shakespeare writes *The Merchant of Venice*

1596

Shakespeare writes *King John;* second three books of Spenser's *The Faerie Queene* published (Spenser died in 1599, leaving the work unfinished)

c. 1596

The Swan theater is built

1597

Shakespeare writes *1 Henry IV*

1598

Beginning of Irish Rebellion; Shakespeare writes *2 Henry IV* and *Much Ado About Nothing;* Jonson writes *Every Man in His Humour;* George Chapman writes Part II of Marlowe's poem *Hero and Leander*

1599

Globe theater opens; Shakespeare writes *Henry V, As You Like It, Julius Caesar,* and *The Merry Wives of Windsor;* Jonson writes *Every Man Out of His Humour*

1600

The Fortune theater opens

1600–1601

Shakespeare writes *Hamlet, Twelfth Night,* and *Troilus and Cressida*

1602

Shakespeare writes *Othello*

1603

Queen Elizabeth I dies, succeeded by King James VI of Scotland, who becomes King James I of England; England sets down the Irish Rebellion; plague in London; Shakespeare writes *All's Well That Ends Well*; Jonson writes *Sejanus*; Lord Chamberlain's Men renamed King's Men

1604

Shakespeare writes *Measure for Measure*; John Marston writes *The Malcontent*; Jonson, Marston, and Chapman collaborate on *Eastward Ho!*

1605

Gunpowder Plot to kill King James I and members of Parliament fails; Marston writes *The Dutch Courtezan*

1606

Shakespeare writes *King Lear* and *Macbeth*; Jonson writes *Volpone*

1607

Founding of Jamestown in America

1607–1609

Shakespeare writes *Antony and Cleopatra, Coriolanus,* and *Timon of Athens* (unfinished), completes *Pericles*

1608

Plague in London; John Webster writes *The White Devil*

1610

Shakespeare writes *Cymbeline*; Jonson writes *The Alchemist*

1610–1611

Shakespeare writes *The Winter's Tale*

1611

Shakespeare writes *The Tempest*

1612–1613

Shakespeare writes *Henry VIII*, possibly with John Fletcher

1613

Globe theater burns down during a performance of *Henry VIII*; Shakespeare and Fletcher collaborate on *The Two Noble Kinsmen*

1614

Jonson writes *Bartholomew Fair;* Webster writes *The Duchess of Malfi*

1616

Shakespeare dies

1623

Actors Henry Condell and John Heminge publish the First Folio, a collection of Shakespeare's plays

FOR FURTHER RESEARCH

ABOUT ELIZABETHAN DRAMATISTS

Leonard Barkan, ed., *Renaissance Drama, New Series X: Comedy.* Evanston, IL: Northwestern University Press, 1980.

Harold Bloom, ed., *Modern Critical Views: Elizabethan Dramatists.* New York: Chelsea House, 1986.

Harold Bloom, *Shakespeare: The Invention of the Human.* New York: Riverhead Books, 1998.

M.C. Bradbrook, *Aspects of Dramatic Form in the English and the Irish Renaissance: The Collected Papers of Muriel Bradbrook, Volume 3.* Totowa, NJ: Barnes & Noble Books, 1983.

John Russell Brown and Bernard Harris, eds., *Stratford-Upon-Avon Studies 9: Elizabethan Theatre.* New York: St. Martin's Press, 1967.

Douglas Cole, *Christopher Marlowe and the Renaissance of Tragedy.* Westport, CT: Greenwood Press, 1995.

Clifford Davidson, C.J. Gianakaris, and John H. Stroupe, eds., *Drama in the Renaissance: Comparative and Critical Essays.* New York: AMS Press, 1986.

Madeleine Doran, *Endeavors of Art: A Study of Form in Elizabethan Drama.* Madison: University of Wisconsin Press, 1954.

Juliet Dusinberre, *Shakespeare and the Nature of Women.* London: Macmillan Press, 1975.

Philip Edwards, Inga-Stina Ewbank, and G.K. Hunter, eds., *Shakespeare's Styles: Essays in Honour of Kenneth Muir.* Cambridge, England: Cambridge University Press, 1980.

Germaine Greer, *Shakespeare.* Oxford, England: Oxford University Press, 1986.

G.R. Hibbard, ed., *The Elizabethan Theatre VI: Papers Given at the Sixth International Conference on Elizabethan Theatre Held at the University of Waterloo, Ontario, in July 1975*. Hamden, CT: Archon, 1978.

Lisa Jardine, *Still Harping on Daughters: Women and Drama in the Age of Shakespeare*. New York: Columbia University Press, 1989.

E.F.C. Ludowyk, *Understanding Shakespeare*. Cambridge, England: Cambridge University Press, 1962.

H.A. Mason, *Shakespeare's Tragedies of Love: An Examination of the Possibility of Common Readings of* Romeo and Juliet, Othello, King Lear *&* Anthony and Cleopatra. London: Chatto and Windus Ltd., 1970.

J.C. Maxwell, ed., *Elizabethan and Jacobean Drama: Critical Essays by Peter Ure*. Liverpool, England: Liverpool University Press, 1974.

William Meyers, "Shakespeare, Shylock, and Dr. Lopez," *Commentary*, April 1996.

Robert S. Miola, *Shakespeare and Classical Tragedy: The Influence of Seneca*. Oxford, England: Clarendon Press, 1992.

Margaret Loftus Ranald, *Shakespeare and His Social Context: Essays in Osmotic Knowledge and Literary Interpretation*. New York: AMS Press, 1987.

Lawrence F. Rhu, "Renewing the Renaissance and Its Literature," *World & I*, December 1998. Available from 3600 New York Ave. NE, Washington, DC 20002.

Mary Beth Rose, ed., *Renaissance Drama, New Series XVII: Renaissance Drama and Cultural Change*. Evanston, IL: Northwestern University Press, 1986.

A.L. Rowse, *Shakespeare the Man*. New York: Harper & Row, 1973.

Robert Sandler, ed., *Northrop Frye on Shakespeare*. New Haven, CT: Yale University Press, 1986.

Samuel Schoenbaum, *Shakespeare: His Life, His English, His Theater*. New York: Signet Classic, 1990.

Elmer Edgar Stoll, *Shakespeare Studies: Historical and Comparative in Method*. New York: Frederick Ungar Publishing, 1960.

Gary Taylor, *Reinventing Shakespeare: A Cultural History, from the Restoration to the Present*. New York: Weidenfeld & Nicolson, 1989.

Alwin Thaler and Norman Sanders, eds., *Shakespearean Essays*. Knoxville: University of Tennessee Press, 1964.

Elliot H. Tokson, *The Popular Image of the Black Man in English Drama, 1550–1688*. Boston: G.K. Hall, 1982.

T.B. Tomlinson, *A Study of Elizabethan and Jacobean Tragedy*. Cambridge, England: Cambridge University Press, 1964.

Albert H. Tricomi, ed., *Early Drama to 1600*. Binghamton: Center for Medieval and Early Renaissance Studies, State University of New York at Binghamton, 1987.

Glynne Wickham, *Shakespeare's Dramatic Heritage: Collected Studies in Medieval, Tudor and Shakespearean Drama*. New York: Barnes & Noble, 1969.

F.P. Wilson, *Marlowe and the Early Shakespeare*. Oxford, England: Clarendon Press, 1953.

ABOUT ELIZABETHAN THEATERS AND TIMES

John Astington, *English Court Theatre, 1558–1642*. New York: Cambridge University Press, 1999.

S.P. Cerasano and Marion Wynne-Davies, eds., *Gloriana's Face: Women, Public and Private, in the English Renaissance*. New York: Harvester Wheatsheaf, 1992.

Alan C. Dessen, *Elizabethan Drama and the Viewer's Eye*. Chapel Hill: University of North Carolina Press, 1977.

Andrew Gurr, *The Shakespearean Stage, 1574–1642*. Cambridge, England: Cambridge University Press, 1992.

——, *The Shakespearian Playing Companies*. Oxford, England: Clarendon Press, 1996.

Hubert Hall, *Society in the Elizabethan Age*. London: S. Sonnenschein, Lowrey & Co., 1902.

Lisa Hopkins, *Queen Elizabeth I and Her Court*. London: Vision Press, 1990.

Norman L. Jones, *The Birth of the Elizabethan Age: England in the 1560s*. Oxford, England: B. Blackwell, 1993.

Scott McMillin, *The Queen's Men and Their Plays*. Cambridge, England: Cambridge University Press, 1998.

J.E. Neale, *Essays in Elizabethan History*. London: J. Cape, 1958.

A.L. Rowse, *The England of Elizabeth: The Structure of Society.* Madison: University of Wisconsin Press, 1950.

A.L. Rowse and George B. Harrison, *Queen Elizabeth and Her Subjects.* Freeport, NY: Books for Libraries Press, 1970.

Andrew Sinclair, *Sir Walter Raleigh and the Age of Discovery.* New York: Penguin, 1984.

Jeffrey L. Singman, *Daily Life in Elizabethan England.* Westport, CT: Greenwood Press, 1995.

Lacey Baldwin Smith, *The Elizabethan World.* Boston: Houghton Mifflin, 1966.

Alison Weir, *The Life of Elizabeth I.* New York: Ballantine, 1998.

INDEX